BEWARE OF

ANGELS

Deceptions in the last days

Books by Roger J. Morneau

A Trip Into the Supernatural
Incredible Answers to Prayer
More Incredible Answers to Prayer
When You Need Incredible Answers to Prayer
The Incredible Power of Prayer

Videos

Incredible Answers to Prayer
A Trip Into the Supernatural

To order, call 1-800-765-6955.
Visit us at http://www.rhpa.org

BEWARE OF

ANGELS

Deceptions in the last days

ROGER
MORNEAU

REVIEW AND HERALD® PUBLISHING ASSOCIATION
HAGERSTOWN, MD 21740

This book was
Edited by Gerald Wheeler
Copyedited by James Cavil
Photo illustration by Matthew Pierce
Cover designed by Matthew Pierce
Interior designed by Patricia S. Wegh
Typeset: 11/13 Garamond 3

PRINTED IN U.S.A.

05 04 03 02   8 7 6 5

R&H Cataloging Service
Morneau, Roger J.
      Beware of angels: deceptions
in the last days.

        1. Angels.   2. Eschatology.   I. Title.

            235.4

ISBN 0-8280-1300-4

CONTENTS

PREFACE

It was only after much prayer and meditation that I decided to write this book. For a number of weeks the words of the apostle Paul to the Colossians kept repeating themselves to my mind: "Let no man beguile you [cheat you] of your reward in a voluntary humility and worshipping of angels" (Col. 2:18).

Yes, Jesus' enemies, Satan and his fallen angels, are at it again in this day and age, misleading and bringing under their control quite a number of God's commandment-keeping people. In fact, two sisters, fourth-generation Adventists, are presently incarcerated in a women's prison in Oregon as a result of angels supposedly coming from God's throne of grace and leading them to kill two persons with a .38-caliber revolver.

In addition to this, friends have brought to my attention similar apparitions of angels in other parts of the world, along with the urgent suggestion that I should write a book to alert God's people to the great danger facing them. But one overpowering factor made it impossible for me to refuse.

As I think about that great day when God will bring the Holy City, the New Jerusalem, to earth, and how after the second resurrection has taken place the redeemed will stand on the walls of the city looking down upon the lost, what a shock it would be for me to hear someone shout, "Roger Morneau, you coward, look at me. I am in this hopeless situation because you kept your mouth shut and refused to write a book that would have alerted me and others to the fact that Satan was determined to cheat us of our eternal reward through deception. You should be here with us, Roger."

By the grace of God dispensed so preciously by His Holy Spirit, this much-needed book is here for you to read. God bless.

–Roger J. Morneau

Acknowledgments

I have pleasure in acknowledging my debt of gratitude to those who spent many hours compiling the reference material I needed so that I could write accurately about the circumstances and events depicted in this book.

My precious and wonderful wife, Hilda, actually spent seven months classifying more than 1,900 pages (23 pounds) of reference material on this case, consisting of police reports, court transcripts, newspaper articles, etc.

I greatly appreciate the help of my computer analyst and good friend, Mike Nelson, in securing newspaper releases on the *Halstead* case from the news media. He spent many, many hours obtaining various materials from the University of Oregon's Knight Library at Eugene, and from the California State Library in Sacramento, where he examined microfilm records during a period of several weeks. Thoughtful assistance was also received from the Pacific Union College Library in Angwin, California.

I wish to express appreciation to Luella Nelson, who helped with typing large parts of the court transcripts into my computer.

While I delight over all those whose help I have mentioned here, there is one more person I wish to thank. My friend Mitch Strong, of Batavia, New York, provided several hundred dollars to secure a 209-page court transcript that had never been released before. It took five months to obtain the material, but it was a tremendous help in my writing project.

For the great amount of help given me here, I say thank you, and God bless.

DEDICATION

I dedicate this book to Mrs. Jodi Halstead, the mother of Sharon Lee Halstead and Deborah Lynne Halstead, whom I admire for two important reasons. First, for her never-failing devotion to her daughters, although they have disappointed her greatly in committing unspeakable crimes.

Second, she is to be admired for her diligent efforts to secure help and guidance from spiritual leaders who were able to help her girls regain their faith in God even after they had totally given up on Him and no longer prayed.

CHAPTER ONE

MURDER BY DECREE

I t was the most difficult thing I had done in my life to please God," Sharon Lee Halstead said as she looked me straight in the eye across a table in the women's penitentiary at Salem, Oregon, on April 24, 1996. I silently waited for her to continue.

"As I walked out of the Greenes' house with the smoking gun in my hands, I realized that I had accomplished only half of the assignment the angel of the Lord had ordered me to do. Lynn Greene was dead with a shot in her chest and a second one in her head. Nathaniel, the Greenes' 3-year-old little boy, had been shot in the face, and his father, David Greene, Jr., had managed to escape through a patio door with only a bullet in his back.

"Will God forgive me for having done such a poor job? I thought to myself, believing that He wanted them all dead. *Surely God will understand that I did the best job I could. Besides, I did a great job on Mike Lemke three days earlier when I put three bullets in him. Never again would demons be able to possess the man."*

What horrifying events had led this woman to become a murderer? A murderer who believed that she was doing the will of God? I had come to interview her to find out. Now she tried to explain the unexplainable.

"For a period of five years I was affiliated with a small group of people involved with a deliverance ministry," she told me. "They believed that they had evolved into a higher degree of standing with God and had received the ability to hear and see angels. During that time we had heard that the time would come when God would require that we do many difficult things for

Him. I told God that I would do anything for Him, anything He wanted. But I never thought that the day would come when He would send an angel to tell me to destroy six individuals who had become possessed with demons."

As we talked in a relaxed way about those years that had molded her and prepared her to kill for God, it deeply impressed me how Satan's angels had cleverly impersonated God's angels, convincing Lynn Greene and the others that they brought special messages from God Himself to that little group. And the day came when by that very same means the demons were able to decree murder. Murder of someone who had been their own spokesperson.

LYNN GREENE A PROPHET?

Many individuals had come to consider Lynn Greene as some kind of prophet, because for a number of years she had claimed to see and hear angels. She supposedly had had numerous conversations with Jesus, who declared the little group to be His very special people on earth, and told them that He would use them to accomplish wonders on behalf of His commandment-keeping people during the closing period of earth's history.

During one prayer meeting Lynn received, from what she believed was God's angel, a message that was supposedly designed to encourage some of her followers. "'You are saddened because you wish not to remain here for so long a time,'" she said the being had told her. "'I will brighten your time here with these thoughts of the future. You, Joseph, with your bare hands will hold back the greatest wave from the sea for many to pass under. And Rachel will not burn as the flames rise above . . . and when the fire goes out all will be amazed in that not a hair from her head will be scorched.'" Mrs. Greene interpreted the cryptic message as meaning that she would be burned at the stake, like Joan of Arc.

"'And you, Sharon [Halstead], the shout of your voice will cause the greatest mountain to crumble on your enemies to protect the Lord's people. I see you in the future doing miraculous deeds by yourself. But yes, he that waits for you will draw near when you have been made new. Your angel that stands by you faithfully will give you the strength, knowledge, and wisdom for these things.'"

Then the angel closed his visit by appealing to the group's pride: "'You here in this room know more of the future than any man, woman, or child in this world. Beware of the fortunetellers in the world.'"

As I listened to Sharon Halstead recount her bizarre tale, I realized that the whole experience of bright and beautiful angels telling them that they were God's elite on the face of the earth had been intended to have an intoxicating effect upon their minds. It blinded them to the errors Satan gradually used to lead them to disregard or totally reject such fundamental truths of the Bible as the state of human beings in death and the fact that we are totally mortal and do not possess immortal spirits that go to heaven at death, or that can leave the body while we live on this planet and then travel to other worlds. These men and women were Seventh-day Adventists, but a fascination with angels had caused them to abandon much of their faith. Angels tricked them into accepting such fantastic accounts as this one Sharon told me:

"Dave Greene, Jr., went to his own planet that God gave him . . . it had miniature people and his favorite bonsai trees. The people on the planet were smaller than the bonsai trees. Dave told us that he talked and visited with these little people, and they were taking care of his bonsai trees for him till he could someday be doing it himself. We were told that after Jesus took us to heaven and we had the chance to visit our own planets and other worlds . . . we were informed that each of us could have whatever plants, trees, or animals we wanted on our planet."

THE ALLURE OF SPECIAL GIFTS AND EXPERIENCES

Sharon recounted some of the gifts and abilities that they thought the angels had endowed the little group with. David Greene, for example, thought he had the gift of interpreting dreams and the ability to be able to distinguish what percent of any music was from God or Satan. As a result, he bought his music accordingly.

"On my birthday, November 4, 1984," Sharon said, "we went to the home of some friends to pray and ask the angels questions. After lunch we all went into the living room, and most of us sat on the floor around Lynn. Then we talked to the angels one at a time as they showed up. The week before, an angel had told Lynn that we were to meet here, and that I would receive my birthday gifts from heaven, something that some in the group had prayed that I would get. A girl named Cheryl had received a large cat that when you looked at it one way it appeared to have stripes, but when it moved and you saw it from another angle, it looked like it had shimmering spots like a leopard."

One person received a gift that turned out to be too much for him. "In 1984," Sharon said, "a member of the group named Charles was given the gift of reading minds. One time he sensed what someone was thinking about him, and he didn't like it. Upset, he asked God to remove the ability."

All the experiences were intended to fascinate, to make the group feel that they knew things no one else did, and that they had a special status with God. During the winter of 1984, for example, the Greenes went skiing at Bend, Oregon. "They told me," Sharon said, "that while skiing down the slopes, a young boy angel went skiing with them. He was the youngest angel Lynn said she had ever seen or talked to." Seeing a boy angel may seem silly to some of my readers, but let me assure you that it was serious to them.

The Greenes believed that they had received special knowledge about the angel Gabriel. According to Sharon, "Lynn said that Gabriel was a very strong muscular-looking angel that stood not quite as tall as the other angels, but could if he wanted to. The angel of truth told Lynn that the angels' favorite height to stand is seven feet, but they could make themselves whatever height they wanted. Also, they could grow their hair any length they desired. They could even change the color of the robes they wore, if they were asked to wear a certain color."

Who could resist wanting to know such unusual things? Surely, to have God reveal them to you meant that you were someone special. Sharon Halstead told me how in 1984 "the angel of truth" had supposedly come to Lynn during a prayer-and-question session. Lynn started smiling and said to the being, "Truth, what do you have on your head?" He said he had just returned from a youth rally in Mexico in which he had taken human form and had been a guest speaker. The people had given him a Mexican sombrero. He had it on so that Lynn could see his gift from the people of Mexico.

That same year one of David Greene's angels would pose for him, either with his wings opened or folded, and David would sketch him. "The sketches I saw looked pretty good," Sharon told me. "Lynn could see the angels posing for Dave, also."

During my research for this book I read the 175-page black notebook David and Lynn Greene had kept about their experiences. The police had removed it from their home after Lynn's murder. It stated that during a period of about four years the Greenes entertained in their home what they believed to be many angels. Angels that flattered and impressed—and deceived. Satan led them step by step to accept the most bizarre things—things contrary to everything they had been taught from the Bible. Here are David's own words: "We have met and talked to many [angels] and have made many friends whom we love very much—to date, 160." He recorded the names of most of them. I will use much material from this black notebook in later chapters.

Jesus supposedly visited the Greenes and their followers. Sharon said that in 1984 her cousin Cheryl had moved from Fort Worth, Texas, to live with her in Grants Pass. "She believed like the rest of the group did. One day Lynn came over to our home to pray and ask questions of Jesus. Jesus had given her a message that she was to come to our home because something special was to be given us this day.

"Lynn came over after lunch, and we with five other persons sat around on the floor and prayed for Jesus to come speak to us, to let us know what it was He had for us. (Many times while at Dave and Lynn's place, an angel would appear bringing a spiritual gift from heaven for someone in the group.) In that way many spiritual gifts were given to each of us.

17

"Lynn prayed for Jesus to come down to us. She saw Jesus when He appeared, and said that He was very bright and beautiful and that thousands of angels surrounded Him. When Jesus started talking, Lynn began to repeat to us the message He wanted us to have. I must say here that almost every message given to us by an angel or Jesus was written word-for-word by one of us as Lynn was speaking it. As for myself, there were times when, having written a message, I would read it back to Jesus or to an angel to make sure I had written it correctly, with no words missing.

"This time Jesus went around to each one of us after having talked, and put the seal of God in our hands. Lynn said that it looked like a picture of the second coming of Christ, with all the holy angels bright and beautiful surrounding Him. Because of his work, Dave wasn't there to receive his seal, but that evening after Lynn and he prayed, Jesus came and gave him his seal, and that made him exceedingly happy.

"Lynn was told that the seal of God on your forehead was the last and hardest seal to acquire. Some in the group had already received the seals in their hands and feet and were waiting and longing for the last seal in the forehead. Once you had received the last seal of God, you were sealed for heaven and eternity with Christ, and you could never sin again.

"David Greene, Jr., received the gift of space travel, better known to most people as out-of-body experiences, and he referred to it as 'spiritual travel.' One evening we were all sitting on the floor. Dave stretched out and went to sleep. After a while Lynn asked him, 'Where have you been, Dave?' His reply was 'Oh, I went through the roof and was taken to another planet, where I saw many beautiful things.'"

The Halstead family observed that at times when David was having one of his spiritual exercises, he would sit in the middle of the living room floor and talk in tongues. It reminds me of an incident that happened while I was affiliated with the elite secret society of spirit worshipers I have described in previous books. The group's high priest commented one time that certain religious groups who practiced speaking in tongues did so under the influence of satanic spirits. These spirits, he claimed, actually caused the people to speak profanities to the Creator, and some actually blasphemed His name without being aware of what they were doing. In addition, he stated that all the excitement that takes place at some of their healing services came from the great master (Satan) and his angels.

For about five years those visiting angels charmed the people in Oregon with promises of wonderful things to come, winning their confidence and love. Then they began to lead them into activities forbidden by the Word of God. Under the pretense of getting them ready to help supply great numbers of Sabbathkeepers with money and other things they would need during the time of trouble, they emphasized the fact that God owns our planet and everything on it. But they gave it a satanic twist—that God wanted them to begin transferring objects that belonged to spiritually lost individuals to places where they would be kept for times of need. The angels informed them that they would work with them in doing this special work for God and His people.

David and Lynn Greene's followers recognized that the last days would be troublesome times, and assumed they would need special preparation. The false angels began with a thread of truth. But then they used it to weave a great lie. The Greenes and their followers did not ask themselves how God would really sustain them through the period. They did not search the Bible and the writings of Ellen White. Rather, they jumped to the conclusion that their survival would depend on their own efforts. Instead of letting God supply what they needed when they needed it, they would stockpile material things beforehand. And they did not question whether the God of Scripture would employ the tactics the false angels led them into step by step.

The supernatural beings told them to go to certain stores, take various objects, and carry them out. The fallen angels assured them that no one would see the stolen merchandise, as the angels would make the objects invisible. No one would stop them. As a result, they were able to do the most unbelievable things as the demonic angels worked in their behalf. For instance, a being instructed four of them to go to a certain store on a particular day and make a major haul of large objects. (This took them five trips to accomplish.) Again the supernatural being assured them that no problems would arise, that no one would interfere with their activities. The angels stated that they would cause the men and women's physical appearance to change, as well as the color of their clothing, and that everything they stole would be made invisible. When everything went with great ease, the group began to enjoy working "for God" in this manner. In about six months, according to a police report, they acquired more than $50,000 worth of merchandise from various sources without anyone noticing.

That particular experience served to convince them that without the shadow of a doubt they were completely under the care of God's angels, and that nothing would happen to them, because they were doing His will. The supernatural beings would predict something, and it would happen, apparently confirming their truthfulness, power, and alleged origin from God. But a prophecy coming to pass does not mean that it is prophecy from God. Satan can make false prophecies seem to be fulfilled. And while the Greenes and their followers felt confident and secure in their calling, in reality Satan had blinded their minds, and without realizing it they became involved in worshiping demons.

The apostle Paul described Satan's great power to deceive the human mind: "The god of this world hath blinded the minds of them which believe not, lest the light of the glorious gospel of Christ . . . should shine unto them" (2 Cor. 4:4). What happened to these men and women offers a powerful illustration of exactly that.

One day a few of the Greenes' group assembled in one of the member's homes, asking questions of a visiting angel whom Lynn Greene declared to be radiant with heavenly glory. Someone then asked how one could see and talk to his or her guardian angel. The being told them through Lynn that guardian angels belonged to a different order of angels than it did, and that the two never talked to each other. God's angels in a heaven of love and closeness never speak to each other? Such a statement should have jarred their minds to the realization that something was extremely wrong. But the men and women accepted the angel's words as true. They had let themselves be conditioned to accept each additional error without questioning it. And the day came when they sincerely believed that God wanted them to kill six individuals.

ENSNARED

Before we continue to see how fallen angels deceived a number of Sabbathkeepers to the point that they were willing to kill, I feel it's important to establish the fact that even the wisest individual can be ensnared in the very same way unless he or she is solidly grounded in God's Word.

First, we need to consider the way Satan has dealt with his prospective victims in ages past. Let's look closely at two particular experiences: how Satan deceived the angels in heaven, and how he cheated our first parents of their Eden home.

To the angels of heaven Lucifer enthusiastically told of his great plan to "be like the most High." He imagined himself a powerful ruler over a large area of the universe, the exalted sovereign of myriads of beautiful worlds, and he assured the angels that all who would side with him he would reward with positions of influence and great power.

The Bible describes it in these words: "How art thou fallen from heaven, O Lucifer, son of the morning! . . . For thou hast said in thine heart, I will ascend into heaven, I will exalt my throne above the stars of God: I will sit also upon the mount of the congregation, in the sides of the north: I will ascend above the heights of the clouds; I will be like the most High" (Isa. 14:12-14).

Satan, occupying a high position in the divine administration of God's universe, felt that he could influence and control things in ways that would force the Creator to agree to his demands and make him a monarch over the universe.

So Lucifer, knowing his own motivations, used the desire for gain to attract the other angels to join him in his cause, and he assured everyone that they would enter a higher state of existence. But as we know, the end result was the direct opposite of what he had promised them. Defeat, bondage, and the submission of their lives to the will of a tyrant was to be their experience until ending in a lake of fire.

In deceiving one third of the angels of heaven, Lucifer cheated them of their eternal well-being by getting them to think as he thought, to feel as he felt, and sure enough, they began to act as he wanted them to. And before long they found themselves involved in a rebellion against God that resulted in their expulsion from heaven. Also, God declared that one day they would perish. What a shocking experience that must have been to all of them.

The high priest of the Luciferian spirit worshipers I once belonged to claimed that a great many of those angels suffered some kind of mental breakdown from which they have never recovered. He called them the oppressors because they are obsessed with sowing misery and destruction in human lives as a way of getting even with the Creator for expelling them from heaven (see *A Trip Into the Supernatural* [Hagerstown, Md.: Review and Herald, 1993]).

Satan and his angels, driven out of heaven to our newly created planet, soon realized that their only hope of survival existed in Satan's ability to cheat Adam and Eve of their dominion. He concluded that if he were to use the desire-for-gain approach on the first humans, he could rob them of everything the Creator had given them. So, with a well-matured plan and skillful maneuvering, Satan drew Eve into a pleasant conversation on the subject of self-aggrandizement and the benefits to gain from it.

As you know, Satan became the prince of our world, and his use of the desire-for-gain tactic to mislead people has been one of his most effective deceptions.

SOUNDING AN ALARM

The apostle Paul wrote to the Colossians: "Let no man beguile you [cheat you] of your reward in a voluntary humility and worshipping of angels" (Col. 2:18). I would paraphrase it this way: "Let no man cheat you of your reward by allowing him to lead you to accept teachings of supposed humility that will in reality result in the worshiping of angels, and eternal separation from God."

The apostle to the Gentiles feared lest "false apostles, [and] deceitful workers" (2 Cor. 11:13) mislead those young Christians. And in writing to the Philippians, he didn't go easy on the deceitful when he said: "Beware of dogs, beware of evil workers" (Phil. 3:2). Again he warned the Corinthians of spiritual corruption and of its danger in these words: "I fear, lest by any means, as the serpent beguiled Eve through his subtilty, so your minds should be corrupted from the simplicity [sincerity] that is in Christ" (2 Cor. 11:3).

Satan's angels seek to prevent you from entering the New Jerusalem. And that will be an overwhelming surprise to vast numbers of Christians who for years had planned to walk the streets of gold in the City of God. I have concluded that after the second resurrection we will find three distinct groups of people thronging outside the walls of the New Jerusalem: the ungodly, the wicked, and the deceived.

The ungodly will be those who had no interest in God in this present world, and lived only for self. The wicked will be those who practiced a lifestyle of deliberate evil, blasphemed God, and actually found pleasure in being vicious criminals. The deceived assumed that they were doing the right thing, but never really checked it against God's Word. They are the ones Paul mentions as losing their eternal reward.

God deeds that reward to a person when he or she accepts Christ as one's Lord and Saviour. It consists of three beautiful promises. The first is that if a person who receives it dies in Christ, God will raise him or her from the dead when Jesus comes in the clouds of heaven. The second promise is that at the resurrection the person will receive an immortalized body that will be untouched by suffering of any kind. And last, life never ending awaits those in the earth made new.

"There, immortal minds will contemplate with never-failing delight the wonders of creative power, the mysteries of redeeming love. There will be no cruel, deceiving foe to tempt to forgetfulness of God. Every faculty will be developed, every capacity increased. The acquirement of knowledge will not weary the mind or exhaust the energies. There the grandest enterprises may be carried forward, the loftiest aspirations reached, the highest ambitions realized; and still there will arise new heights to surmount, new wonders to admire, new truths to comprehend, fresh objects to call forth the powers of mind and soul and body" *(The Great Controversy,* p. 677).

FALSE CHRISTS AND FALSE PROPHETS

Matthew's Gospel tells us that on a certain day as Jesus sat on the Mount of Olives, His disciples asked: "What shall be the sign of thy coming, and of the end of the world?" (Matt. 24:3). Jesus' precise reply centered on the great danger of being deceived, or, in other words, of being cheated out of eternal life. "Jesus answered and said unto them, Take heed that no man deceive you. For many shall come in my name, saying, I am Christ; and shall deceive many" (verses 4, 5).

"There shall arise false Christs, and false prophets, and shall shew great signs and wonders; insomuch that, if it were possible, they shall deceive the very elect" (verse 24).

In the vast numbers of letters that I receive, many individuals ask me when I think that the false christs and false prophets Jesus said would come before His second advent will begin to arrive? And in talking over the phone with some of those individuals, they seem stunned with disbelief when I tell them that great numbers of false christs and false prophets have already been actively practicing their deceptions in the religious world for decades.

You see, when a beautiful angel appears to a person and claims to come from the throne of God, then speaks a message not in harmony with the Word of God, and the recipient turns around and encourages people to accept such a message as a means of getting closer to God, I consider that individual a false prophet in the fullest sense of the word. Also, when a person tells of seeing Jesus arriving with a retinue of beautiful angels, and that He is moving among their particular little group blessing them, and at the same time the individual declares things that contradict God's Holy Word, you can rest assured that a false christ, one of Satan's angels, is at work.

It was during the mid-1970s that I became aware that the fallen cherubim and his spirit associates were developing new avenues to condition vast numbers of people to accept the popular belief of life after death, and to reject the biblical teaching that "the dead know not any thing" (Eccl. 9:5, 6). At that time television talk shows were coming into existence, and the most notable ones were *The PTL Club,* hosted by Jim and Tammy Bakker; *The 700 Club,* hosted by Pat Robertson, and the *Merv Griffin Show.*

At that same time I was division sales manager in telephone directory advertising sales (yellow pages) for the Continental Telephone System in the northeastern United States. In the evening in my motel room, while processing a great deal of paperwork, I used to view one or two of those shows, depending on the topic. My interest especially centered on anything relating to the time of the end and the second coming of Christ. In addition, I watched for so-called near-death experiences in which people supposedly died and went to a land of glory. Then an angel, or a longtime dead relative, or at times supposedly even Jesus Himself, would tell them to return to earth to take up their bodies again and live to help others prepare for that land of glory.

(I kept notes on many of these types of programs, which is why I can describe them now. My wife asked me at the time why I was doing it, and I had no idea. Never did I imagine that I would be using them in a book.)

The high priest of the spiritist society I had once belonged to had described them to me decades before. He claimed that spirits produced them in the minds of certain individuals by moving upon their imagination to create scenes so vivid that they became impressed upon their minds during unconsciousness. Once awake and alert, such persons sincerely believed that their experience had been real. "Many of those persons," the priest assured me, "become powerful workers for the master [Satan], who never ceases to attract people to his cause." Again, I consider these deceived individuals to be false prophets.

Merv Griffin had a fascination with the supernatural, and on his show interviewed a lot of people who had interesting encounters with the supposed spirits of the dead. For instance, on November 14, 1978, I was in Concord, New Hampshire, watching his show as he interviewed Lillian Carter, President Carter's mother, and the country singer Loretta Lynn. During the discussion he mentioned to Mrs. Carter that Loretta Lynn was living in a haunted house. Loretta explained that the experience had been beneficial to her family. "The ghosts are friendly," she said. "The children have seen some of them and have no fear of them." She said that they had carpeted the staircase because they heard footsteps as the ghosts went up and down the old staircase. In addition, doors opened and closed by themselves, and at times the lights turned on and off, but she refused to get rid of the spirits.

I thought to myself, *If she realized that Satan's angels were dwelling in her home so as to shut out heaven's blessings, she would cry out for help.* Deception is such a sad thing.

AN END-TIME SATANIC DECEPTION

A Richard Battiesta, who was declared legally dead and brought back to life by a team of doctors in a New York City hospital, presented an interesting story on the December 5, 1978, *Merv Griffin Show* (I watched on channel 2 out of Port Jervis, New York). Richard told how he had suffered a cardiac arrest, in which it seemed his soul left his body and traveled to a place of great splendor. There he saw his grandfather coming to greet him. But he was not allowed to stay there, being told that he had to return to earth. He did not want to return to his body, and was most distressed over the fact that the doctors kept working to bring him back to life.

Conscious again, he told everyone that he wanted to die, but his 17-year-old son helped change his mind. Battiesta declared the experience to have been most pleasurable, allowing him to discover what perfect joy and peace was like.

Such experiences profoundly influence those who accept the popular belief that human beings have an immortal soul, and who have never fortified their minds with the Word of God, which declares that God only "hath immortality" (1 Tim. 6:16). That "the dead know not any thing" (Eccl. 9:5, 6). Also, that "the dead praise not the Lord, neither any that go down into silence" (Ps. 115:17). According to the apostle Paul, life after death will take place at the resurrection of the just at Christ's second coming, and not before (see 1 Thess. 4:13-18). It is vital that we fortify our minds by memorizing such passages to avoid being swept away by Satan's deceptions. Deceptions that will more and more convince the world that the dead are in heaven having a wonderful experience.

The high priest of the spiritists described to me more than a half century ago how cleverly Satan's angels have nurtured in humans the belief of life after death. But my interest peaked when he stated that demonic spirits have at certain times assumed human form. Satan himself materialized on the day of Jesus' crucifixion to assure himself that some of the Jewish people would reject the great Preacher, and also to see that the greatest amount of pain and suffering would be brought to bear upon Him whom he had learned to hate when in the courts of heaven.

About a year later, after having accepted Christ as my Lord and Saviour, I read the chapter in *The Desire of Ages* on the crucifixion of Christ. In it I came upon a paragraph that referred to the materialization of Satan's angels. Pilate asked the Jewish people, "'Whom will ye that I release unto you? Barabbas, or Jesus which is called Christ?' Like the bellowing of wild beasts came the answer of the mob, 'Release unto us Barabbas!' Louder and louder swelled the cry, Barabbas! Barabbas! . . . 'What shall I do then with Jesus which is called Christ?' . . . Again the surging multitude roared like demons. *Demons themselves, in human form,* were in the crowd, and what could be expected but the answer, 'Let Him be crucified'" (p. 733; italics supplied).

A few pages later I found this additional bit of information: *"Satan with his angels, in human form,* was present at the cross" (pp. 746-749; italics supplied). This author, I thought, had to be inspired to come up with such information known to so few people.

The spiritist high priest himself, though, was puzzled by the idea of spirits materializing. His spirit guide, who had mentioned it to him, left several things unexplained: how they materialize, and why such occurrences were so few and far between. The spirit guide did say, however, that more such incidents would take place as the conflict between Christ and Satan intensifies and draws to a close.

A MATERIALIZED SPIRIT HELPS TELLY SAVALAS

An example of the form such appearances will take is illustrated by a story Telly Savalas, the actor who played the television detective Kojak, told on the *Larry King Live* program in February 1988. One evening, not long after he left military service, he was driving home on Long Island, New York. Unfortunately he ran out of gas on an expressway. A car stopped, and the driver asked if he was OK. When Savalas told him that he was out of gas, the fellow stated that he didn't have the time to drive him to a service station, but if he were to walk a few hundred feet across a patch of trees, he would be on a regular road where he could get help.

So Savalas did as told, and, coming out of the woods onto the road, was surprised to see a black Cadillac. The neatly dressed man at the steering wheel said, "Get in, and I'll take you to a gas station." They chatted along, and as they reached a service station Savalas reached in his back pocket to get his wallet, then realized that he had left it at home. Before he had time to explain, the driver said, "Don't trouble yourself over your wallet. I'll let you have a dollar." In those days you could get three gallons of gas for that small amount of money.

Returning to where he had picked Savalas up, the man dominated the conversation, and somehow Savalas was not able to ask how he happened to be waiting in his Cadillac or how he knew that Savalas had forgotten his wallet. Getting out of the car, Savalas asked the man if he would write his name, address, and phone number on a piece of paper, as he was going to send him the dollar in the mail. The fellow wrote his address in New Jersey, added that the phone number was that of a tavern he frequented often, then pulled away.

A couple days later Savalas called the number and asked to talk to a Robert Blenk, if he happened to be there. The person at the end of the line said, "I will have you talk to his wife." The first thing she said was "What kind of joke is this?" Savalas told her about the experience he had. Then she asked him to describe the man and his car, and how he was dressed. Then the woman started to cry and said, "The person you have described is exactly what my husband looked like. He had a black Cadillac, and when he died two years ago, he was buried wearing a gray suit with that same pattern you told me about."

The experience made a profound impression on Telly Savalas. Previously he had never been interested in spiritual things, but now he found himself a firm believer in the immortality of the soul and life after death. As an entertainer he had had wonderful opportunities to tell his story to great numbers of people, and had never passed up an opportunity to speak about the subject.

Savalas's story perfectly illustrates how demonic spirits materialize to reinforce fallacies that will powerfully ensnare vast numbers of people during the closing of earth's history.

During the late 1970s certain evangelical Christians became fascinated with what they referred to as "new light," teachings they felt had been withheld from Christians for too long a time. So they started to press God to give them such "new light." Other individuals became obsessed with the idea that the time was right to supplicate God for the privilege of seeing and talking with angels that could instruct them in new and better ways of serving Him.

Too often a desire for self-exaltation motivated such desires, as the future revealed, and opened the way for Satan's angels to appear to certain persons claiming to come from heaven itself. Gradually such beings went about perverting the gospel of Christ. As I saw such a trend taking place in some of the Sunday churches, I wondered how long it would take for demonic spirits to infiltrate the thinking of God's commandment-keeping people in a similar way. It didn't take very long, as you will see in upcoming chapters.

Also during the early 1980s an exciting new phenomenon

began to take place in some Protestant circles. Some of their members considered themselves as demon-possessed, and the spiritual leaders who in reality had unwittingly set the people up to become demon-possessed lost no time in declaring themselves experts at solving such problems. They held exorcism services lasting at times as long as 12 to 16 hours in order to rid a person of dozens of "demons." The exorcist would command the spirits, one at a time, to identify themselves and to answer numerous questions about their occupation, their various activities, etc.

One Baptist minister in Chicago became famous overnight for his exploits into the supernatural. It attracted the news media's attention and gave him national exposure of the type that one could not buy with a million dollars. Ministers from various denominations flocked to him to hear about his "spiritual discovery," and along with them were three or four Seventh-day Adventists. I need to add here that none of the leaders of the Seventh-day Adventist Church had anything to do with that spiritual excitement.

The way was being opened for Satan's lying spirits to do a work that would be clothed in mysticism, and that would result in great numbers of people losing faith in Christ's power to save. Many would never recover, and would lose out on eternal life.

CHAPTER TWO

REFUSING
TO GET INVOLVED

efore we continue Sharon Halstead's story, I need to relate the circumstances that led me to see her in prison and write this book—a book I had no intention to write, and had resisted for a number of years. The events began many years before.

In February of 1990 my first book on prayer came off the press, and a great number of people who had read the story of my conversion experience from spiritism as recorded in *A Trip Into the Supernatural* (first published in 1982) quickly contacted me, hoping to find help in my praying for them.

Either they themselves, a member of their family, a friend of theirs, or some other person was experiencing some form of demonic oppression. Some out of curiosity had started attending services conducted by Adventist exorcists, and since then weird things had begun taking place in their lives.

As I corresponded with those individuals, trying to get them out of their difficulties, I became aware that a great many of them had been victimized by spiritual leaders who did not realize that they were destroying people's faith in Christ's power to save, and were actually delivering people into Satan's power.

Let me illustrate with a brief experience. By September of 1990 letters bringing prayer requests began to arrive daily in large numbers. The number of persons on my prayer list already amounted to hundreds, taking up all my available time. But one letter caught my attention in a special way, and as I read I realized that spirits were constantly harassing the writer. They had determined to wear out her life forces and cause her to destroy herself. I lost no time in phoning her, and in so doing found that she had lived the past six years of her life under most difficult conditions, having been robbed of all hope and faith in God.

"In one hour," Alice told me, "my world was turned upside down, and I have not recovered from the damage." During the mid-1980s she drove to church alone one Sabbath morning. Her daughter was away with her father for the weekend. Alice (not her real name) began thinking how difficult life had become for her when her husband, John, left her for another woman. But now the older children were on their own and doing well in their various occupations, and her teenage daughter was the joy of her life. Alice had just received a new promotion from her employer with a substantial increase in her salary that she praised God for.

Looking at her watch, she pressed down harder on the accelerator to make sure that she would arrive before the 11:00 service. Alice entered the sanctuary just as the elders knelt for prayer and, seeing one open space, sat in the second pew from the rear of the church. She recognized the visiting minister's name in the bulletin. Having heard of some of his activities as an SDA exorcist, she was delighted at the opportunity to hear him talk.

As the speaker told of having delivered wonderful Christians from demon possession, Christians who were not aware that they had been demon-possessed, Alice became distressed over the fact that she was experiencing a great many of the symptoms those persons supposedly had. She had suffered with allergies for many years, but noticed that as she grew older the allergic attacks had diminished considerably. Yes, she had been and still was fearful of a number of things, another symptom the minister claimed to be a sign of demon possession. Especially when the children had been young, she would worry about their getting home safely from school. Quite frequently she had thought of how terrible a thing it would be if her oldest son got into an accident with his old car. And even at her age she was still fearful of riding in someone else's car, but had learned to live with her shortcomings.

As the speaker told during his 45-minute talk of additional cases of "demonized Christians," and of the symptoms they had experienced before he delivered them from Satan's power, Alice became convinced that she was indeed demon-possessed, and began to feel bitter about the fact that Jesus, the one whom she had lived for and trusted with her whole heart, had not been able to keep her from the power of evil spirits. "I actually felt betrayed," she said, "and anger filled my heart. Then I felt a strange feeling of hate toward Christ possessing my being, and it took all the strength I could muster to refrain myself from shouting in the church as loud as I could that Jesus was no Saviour. Then I made the decision to go home and kill myself."

When the service ended, the deacons dismissed the people by rows, but Alice did not get up until only a dozen or so people remained in the church. With the visiting minister was another couple, and the woman came and said, "Dear sister, you look so distressed. Is there something I could help you with?" Alice felt drained of energy and overwhelmed, but slowly, and with great effort, started toward the exit. The woman spoke again, saying, "You look so very troubled; would you like to tell me about it?" Alice unburdened her soul by saying that the preacher's message had made it clear that she was demon-possessed, that Jesus was no Saviour, and that she didn't care to live anymore. The woman assured her that all her problems would be over as soon as the elder conducted an exorcism for her; then she hugged her tightly.

At that moment Alice felt as if a fiery arrow had pierced her heart, and intense heat shot throughout her entire body. She knew for a certainty that she was demon-possessed, as what came out of her mouth were not the words she was trying to say, but other words—words that she had given no thought to.

The visiting minister conducted an exorcism the next day that lasted 16 hours, during which the exorcist claimed to have forced 67 demons out of her. He matched wits with the evil spirits that objected to his demands. After the service Alice was supposedly back to her normal self, but as the days went by she saw her life become a shambles. She became disoriented and plagued with uncertainty, and began having a hard time making decisions. Her prayer life had come to a standstill. No longer able to express appreciation to her Creator for His blessings in her life, she gave up praying. Her $48,000-a-year position went to someone else, as her work skills deteriorated. As I said earlier, she had been robbed of all hope and faith in God, and the results were disastrous.

She told me that someone had given her a copy of *Incredible Answers to Prayer,* she had found comfort and encouragement in reading it, and now she felt that perhaps I could help her regain hope and faith in God. I agreed to that, not thinking that she would be calling me in the middle of the night when the spirits oppressed her. For more than two years she phoned me every weekend and many times in between. The conversations took as long as an hour. I would quote Scripture and expound the Word of God until she regained hope and courage to continue her life.

Sometimes I felt that I was wasting my time in trying to help her, but I wouldn't let such feelings deter me from seeking special help from God in her behalf. While she was talking I would silently reach out to God the Father, pleading the merits of the shed blood of Christ as the reason His Holy Spirit should minister redemption and healing, then grant her peace, contentment, and solid comfort in Christ. I based my response on what Ellen White had written about the part God's Holy Spirit plays in our heavenly Father's perfect plan of salvation.

For instance, before going to the cross, Jesus sought to inspire His disciples with the fact that when He would no longer be with them, they would have the presence and wonder-working power of the Holy Spirit. *The Desire of Ages* tells us that our Lord experienced great joy over the way the Spirit of God would work for helpless humanity after His departure. "The Spirit was to be given as a regenerating agent, and without this the sacrifice of Christ would have been of no avail." Also, "sin could be resisted and overcome only through the mighty agency of the Third Person of the Godhead, who would come with no modified energy, but in the fullness of divine power" (p. 671).

Every time those inspiring words come to mind, it never fails that I hear Paul's words to Titus telling us that we are saved by the washing of regeneration and the renewing of the Holy Spirit (see Titus 3:5).

So it is that for the past 49 years of my Christian walk I have looked on the Holy Spirit as possessing the "divine power to overcome all hereditary and cultivated tendencies to evil" in a person's life, and to sustain one in rightdoing *(ibid.).* And today people who have read my books have arrived at the same understanding, having experienced in their own lives the transforming power of the Spirit of God. They have ventured in praying for their wayward sons and daughters to secure for them special grace from God. Many of them write me telling how the Holy Spirit has transformed their loved ones, healing their mental, emotional, and spiritual faculties, and getting their hearts attuned with the heart of God our heavenly Father.

Alice's experience was but one of many from people who have struggled with the supernatural and then, after reading about my own conversion experience from spiritism and my books on prayer, have gotten in touch with me. And as I added my intercessions to theirs, and God's Holy Spirit began to move in their behalf, those individuals saw themselves being redeemed from the power of Satan and restored to living for Christ. As the Spirit of God restored their minds, they began to understand also how extremism and fanaticism had crippled their intelligence and led them into spiritual bondage. Many also began urging me to write a book on the supernatural that would help people recognize the working of demonic spirits before they fell into their snares.

After having given the matter a great deal of thought, I refused to get involved that way. Realizing that it would take a number of months to complete such a project, and that my prayer ministry would have to take second place, I decided against it. I felt that taking the time to write such a work would cancel out a great part of the work that I had asked God to keep me alive to do.

PLEASE HELP US

In mid-January 1991 I received a letter that came from halfway around the world. It had an urgent request for help. Here are a few excerpts from it, and as usual I have changed the names.

"Dear Mr. Morneau,

"Although we are sure you must have many requests from many different people for prayer on their behalf, we'd like, in light of this special gift that God has blessed you with, to ask you if you would mind adding our names to your prayer list, as we feel a very real need of God in our lives.

"We were both born into Seventh-day Adventist families, and are both baptized members of the church. However, because of many circumstances, we feel our faith is wavering.

"About seven years ago, before I knew her, Jennifer suffered a nervous breakdown from the many serious pressures in her life at the time. Since that time several other circumstantial elements have prevented her from recovering sufficiently, some of them in fact worsening the problem. Jennifer is almost continually in a state of severe depression and torment, and medical professionals have not been able to help.

"Several pastors that we have approached seem to be of the opinion that there may be satanic involvement, as several unexplained and unfortunate incidents have occurred. We feel that not just our marriage and our earthly lives are at stake, but also our eternal ones as well, and as we are very worried about it, we beg you to intercede with God on our behalf.

"We thank you for taking the time to read this letter, and we look forward to hearing from you soon.

"Yours faithfully,
Kevin and Jennifer B."

As soon as I received the letter I presented it before the Lord, imploring His grace for them and setting forth in great detail the distress and perplexity that had swamped their lives. My intercessions in their behalf were constant, but as the months went by there seemed no change for the better, as letters kept coming. In fact, things were getting worse, as Jennifer had developed a stomach ulcer that began to bleed frequently.

I realized that demonic spirits were at work here, that they were especially attacking Jennifer, but I couldn't put a finger on their avenue of access. So one day I asked the Lord to help me understand the origin of their problem, what it was that allowed the forces of evil to operate as openly as they did. Shortly afterward, in August of that year, I received a letter from Kevin describing some experiences that had almost driven Jennifer out of her mind.

Every time either one of them flushed their toilet, she would experience excruciating head pain even if she blocked her ears. So to help the situation, they drank only two glasses of water per day and ate as little as possible, which resulted in their being hungry, thirsty, and constantly uncomfortable.

"Her life," he said, "is a living nightmare." Before closing, he asked, "Do you think the way to get help from God is to get Jennifer anointed?" In my reply I didn't encourage him to do so since I have had no experience in that type of situation.

Another few weeks went by; then I received a letter from Jennifer's father, who felt that I needed a better understanding of how his daughter had become as sick as she had. Here are some excerpts from his letter:

"About seven years ago our family moved from a country town, where our three children had been schooled, to a capital city. The education system was very different, and for Jennifer the system was much more permissive. She found it very difficult to adapt. After 10 months her concentration lapsed and her studies suffered. She had previously been very successful academically. We don't know why this happened; it may have been the change, or perhaps some event occurred that she has never talked about."

After giving additional information, telling how Jennifer had suffered a nervous breakdown, he added, "We took her to doctors and therapists and counselors and psychiatrists, and she developed an aversion for these professionals that has become quite phobic, so that now she is unable to face the thought of any medical treatment, refusing even to take any medication."

A couple weeks later the father phoned me with what he considered a brilliant suggestion. His daughter felt that if she were to come to the United States, visit us in Endicott, New York, and get anointed by our pastor, she would be healed. I explained to him that such an undertaking would be costly to begin with, since they would have to fly thousands of miles in each direction. Besides, we couldn't be sure of her being healed. To my great surprise, he declared that the cost of the trip wouldn't be a problem for them (the families of the couple, I discovered, were extremely wealthy), and regardless of the outcome, he would feel good about it. Then he asked if I could see the young couple in two weeks.

The day they arrived in town I called my pastor to make arrangements to have an anointing service in two or three days. I had not yet met the young man, new to our area, since he had arrived just two days before, and I ran into some difficulties. First of all, he was reluctant to anoint a person whom he knew nothing about, especially one coming from a foreign country. And when I told him that we had intended to have the service in our home because of my heart condition, and that I would like to join the elders in prayer for the young woman, he lost no time in checking my background.

"Are you presently an elder in this local church?" he asked. I explained that I was not, but that I had been ordained to that office in the early sixties, and had been the first elder of a local congregation for many years.

"Well, I don't think you can take part in this service, but I will have to check with the New York Conference president, who happens to be in Perth, Australia, attending Annual Council. I will telephone him tomorrow."

My heart sank at the thought that Kevin and Jennifer might have to return home without an anointing service. That night I pleaded with God to intervene in some way so that the young couple's shaky Christian experience would not be damaged to the point that they'd give up on religion altogether.

During the next day, news came that the New York Conference president had given his blessing to go ahead with the anointing service. But I could detect some reluctance on the part of the pastor, who felt obligated to comply with a decision he didn't believe in. While the anointing service didn't produce immediate improvement in Jennifer's condition, a great deal of new information surfaced during the three days they visited. Finally I learned the way the demonic spirits had gained control of her life.

After arriving in Endicott in late afternoon and checking into a motel, Kevin phoned to inform us that the trip had gone well. We invited the couple to eat with us. The next morning he gave us a ring to say that he would be a bit late, and that Jennifer couldn't make it, as she was experiencing some distress. As we conversed that morning I listened for anything that would reveal how the spirits had succeeded in reaching his wife. My prayer to understand their dilemma received its answer when he told us about their honeymoon.

Arriving at their destination in a large city, they had seen billboards, placards, and other advertising telling about some popular American rock artists performing at a large stadium. The idea of attending the concert thrilled Jennifer, but Kevin had decided to stop listening to that kind of music, and to get closer to God. Then he thought to himself, *Our honeymoon is such a special occasion. I should do everything I can to make my bride happy.* So he bought tickets.

Jennifer was overjoyed with the performance, and declared the experience one of the high days in her life. Then something strange began to take place. The next morning she woke up feeling a bit depressed but couldn't associate the way she felt with anything in particular. As they traveled in their car that day to see the city, a motorcycle pulled in front of them. On the cyclist's jacket were the words "Harley-Davidson" in large letters. Instantly Jennifer went into deep depression and began to weep, and continued in that state for most of the day.

A few days later Kevin discovered that Jennifer reacted the same way whenever she saw the word "green" on a sign, a building, a vehicle, or anything else. Both "Harley" and "green" triggered agonizing bouts of depression, so when she rode in the car with her husband and they passed through a town, she would stare down at the floor to avoid seeing the words. Once out of town she could look up again.

Jennifer's problem had begun after she attended the heavy metal rock concert. Decades earlier the spiritist high priest had told me that when Christians enter areas where occult practitioners dabble, God's angels have to stay out. He explained that evil angels seek to break through God's protection around an individual. They influence the person to visit a fortuneteller, an astrologer, a hypnotist, or anyone involved in an occult practice. In my estimation Satan uses rock concerts as direct avenues to lure carefree young people, through the popularity of the music and the fact that some musicians like to experiment with the occult as a way of achieving fame and success, into relinquishing power and control to demonic spirits.

As Kevin and Jennifer visited us one day in Endicott I noticed that she had a small cassette player in her shoulder bag with a fine wire leading to her left ear. The next morning Kevin stopped by, and since he was alone I asked him about the cassette player. He explained that listening to her favorite music calmed Jennifer, and she experienced far fewer problems. Then I urged him to be completely honest with me as I asked, "Is Jennifer listening to rock music?"

Somewhat surprised, he replied, "I had hoped that you wouldn't ask me that question. Yes, Mr. Morneau, I am sorry to say that she does listen to rock music as a way of soothing her nerves."

I explained to Kevin that demonic spirits had used the music to take control of his wife's mental and emotional faculties, and intended to drive her to an early grave.

Realizing that an intense struggle with the forces of evil lay ahead of them, I assured him that our intercessions in their behalf would be constant. At the same time I made it clear that Jennifer would have to give up rock music before she could escape the evil forces. The outcome rested on how she would use the freedom of choice that God has given to all human beings, and that He respects even when we make bad choices. As long as people cherish something demonic spirits have used to establish control over them, be it rock music or anything else, they show what power they allow to rule over them.

Refusing to Get Involved

The young couple returned to their native country, and as the months passed the news from them grew even more discouraging. One letter said that "Jennifer's condition is worsening, with enormous suffering." Another one read: "I am desperately worried about Jennifer's physical health, as she is experiencing terrible headaches, and her stomach ulcer has worsened drastically and bleeds internally from time to time. She feels that a power is taking hold of her, and she then has terrible urges to take a knife and cut me up in pieces while I am sleeping. Also, at times she feels like drowning our little dog, whom we love very much."

As I pondered the whole thing in my mind I concluded that the spirits were about to attack her physically, so I prayed for God to deliver her from destruction if such a thing should happen to her. Not long after that, I received a phone call from Kevin, who was greatly disturbed about something. Then a few days later I received a letter from him giving greater details on the incident.

One morning he heard Jennifer fall in the bathroom and rushed to her just in time to see her facedown on the floor and struggling "while her head was being bashed up and down against the floor, her body held with one arm behind her back by some invisible being. Blood was pouring from her nose." Immediately Kevin said, "Dear Jesus, please help!" At once the attack stopped. He picked her up, and saw black bruises and finger marks on one arm, on one shoulder, and on part of her scalp, where something had pulled her hair.

After the bleeding stopped and Jennifer regained her composure, she described the ordeal. As she was walking toward the bathroom she felt an invisible presence and began struggling with it. Something twisted an arm behind her back and threw her down. Then the invisible forced grabbed her hair to bash her head against the ceramic-tiled floor.

Kevin told me that the incident convinced Jennifer to give up rock music. Intercessory prayer in her behalf, claiming the blood Jesus shed on Calvary as the reason He should answer our prayers, brought Jesus' redeeming power into her life, and before long she was of sound mind and body.

They now have a beautiful child who has brought great joy into their lives, and for whom they thank God greatly. As I look over Kevin's letters from those difficult days, I notice that he never failed to say, "Please help us with your intercessions!" And God did.

PRESSED INTO SERVICE

The two experiences that I have just recounted demonstrate how the forces of evil are gaining access to God's commandment-keeping people in an attempt to separate them from God, and how they intend to destroy them. I am receiving letters from all over the world telling of similar experiences with the supernatural. This past year the number of letters has at least doubled that of the previous five years.

As I said earlier, I didn't want to write a book on deceptions of the last days. My whole life revolves around praying for people. I have at present more than 17,000 persons on my prayer list, and I refuse to let anything divert my attention from that vital responsibility. Besides, I convinced myself that if the Lord wanted such a book written at this time He knew a lot of people who could do a much better job at it than someone who never had a day of formal English schooling in his life.

I had been born and raised in a French-speaking area of eastern Canada and for a long time assumed that the opportunity to learn the English language had passed me by forever. Then World War II came and transplanted me to the Montreal area, where I signed up with the merchant navy. In it I met English-speaking people for the first time in my life. But I didn't apply myself to learning the language until about 1950, after having been married to Hilda for about three years. I learned so we could go to the United States in order to give our two children more advantages in life than we had had.

When I told Hilda of my intentions, she thought it was great, but saw one big obstacle blocking the way. "How do you intend to earn a living in sales when you know so little English, and can't write it? Besides, your sales work makes it impossible for you to attend evening classes. I can't figure you out."

I replied that I had a plan that would get us to the States in about four years without fail. I had decided to learn English by memorizing words out of the dictionary. With the blessing of the Spirit of God in my life I figured that it would take about four years to grasp the language, then three additional years to polish it. And sure enough—in 1954 we entered the United States with our green cards, became U.S. citizens in 1975, and have enjoyed this God-blessed country for 42 years. And today as I think upon it, I can't help saying, GLORY TO GOD IN THE HIGHEST!

CHAPTER THREE

A RED SEA EXPERIENCE

I n August 1995 I received first a phone call, then a letter, from a Mrs. Jodi Halstead, who resided in Oregon. Her voice carried a sense of urgency, a cry for help. When I answered, she lost no time in saying that she was calling at the urging of Pastor Reginald Robinson, associate speaker of the *Breath of Life* television program.

She explained that she had two daughters incarcerated in a women's prison in Salem, Oregon, for having killed two people during the autumn of 1988. Mrs. Halstead said that one of the girls, Sharon Lee, had been experiencing some oppression from demonic spirits from time to time during the past seven years, but now the spirits were hurting her physically. She needed special help.

Mrs. Halstead stated also that Pastor Robinson had been most helpful to her daughters after their arrest, had visited them in jail, and had helped them adjust to the shock of realizing that the directives given them by the beautiful angels had come not from God, but from Satan and his fallen angels.

When I asked her to describe the supernatural attacks, she explained that the girls had received a set of my four books, and that evening as Sharon Lee was lying on her bed in her prison cell, reading *A Trip Into the Supernatural,* an invisible force tried to pull the book out of her hands. She first heard a high-pitched sound such beings sometimes make as they approach a victim. Previous supernatural visits had alerted her to how they occasionally behave. Realizing that apparently more than one spirit was present, she braced herself and held the book with both hands. "I had the feeling that they would try to shove me off my bed and pull the book from me at the same time, and sure enough, they tried," she told her mother. (Sharon verified much of the information her mother gave me when I visited the sisters in April 1996.)

The spirits had previously manifested their presence to Sharon but had not been physically oppressive. They would touch her hair and make sounds that would keep her from going to sleep. "In the very beginning of those experiences," Sharon said, "the spirits placed me in a relaxed state, and I fell asleep in a few short minutes." At other times they would wake her up as she slept comfortably under two wool blankets by letting cold air seep in around her body. A few minutes later they would surround her bed, pressing the blankets down around her.

Jodi Halstead asked if I would help Sharon Lee. Our phone conversation must have lasted an hour as she recounted some of the events that had led to her daughters' arrest and imprisonment. Then she read me a few lines from a letter she had received recently from Sharon Lee:

"Since August 4 I have been harassed and physically tortured by these spirits. Sometimes they touch me, and I feel as though I have been burned with electricity. One morning I awoke to an evil spirit trying to strangle me and press the air out of my lungs."

Besides talking over the phone with Mrs. Halstead, I sent her a letter telling how we should pray for her daughter, then wrote Sharon Lee to give her some guidance and, above all, direct her to the greatest Source of strength and grace available to her.

"Dear Sharon,
"As you are well aware, your mother has written to me, and we have also conversed over the phone about the disastrous events that have come into your life. I presented your difficulties before the Lord as soon as I learned of them, imploring His grace for you.
"At this time I wish to bring to your attention the fact that I am not an Adventist exorcist. I am a praying man, and the guidance that I can give you centers strictly on Christ Jesus' power to

save through the merits of His divine blood shed on Calvary for our redemption.

"It is a sad thing that demonic spirits have been terrorizing your life, but let me assure you that your security is to be found in the superior power of our great Redeemer.

"Only through the merits of the divine blood of Christ shed on Calvary for our salvation can we escape the harassment of demonic spirits. So I suggest that every day you read about the crucifixion of Christ in Matthew 27:24-54. Then plead with our heavenly Father for the merits of that great sacrifice to be appropriated to you, and that the Holy Spirit may fight your spiritual battles, overthrowing the forces of evil.

"'Earnest, persevering supplications to God in faith . . . can alone avail to bring men the Holy Spirit's aid in the battle against principalities and powers, the rulers of the darkness of this world, and wicked spirits in high places' *(The Desire of Ages,* p. 431).

"I would like to suggest that you make sure that the way is wide open between you and your Creator at all times. To make this a reality, the very first thing to do in the morning when you wake up is to direct your mind to the Holy of Holies of the heavenly sanctuary. And I mean first. Don't get out of bed, talk to anyone, or check the weather report. Address the Lord Jesus silently, if it is not possible to speak to Him audibly. Thank Him for His loving care over you, and for appropriating to you the merits of His sacred divine blood that He shed on Calvary for your salvation.

"I understand that you have my fourth book that came off the press in May, entitled *When You Need Incredible Answers to Prayer.* Read chapter 2, 'Enjoying a Solid Relationship With Christ,' to make sure that your prayers are reaching the throne of God. To help you strengthen your confidence in Christ's power to save, I would suggest that you memorize verses of Scripture that will fortify your faith, such as Colossians 1:14. It declares that in Him, that is Christ, 'we have redemption through his blood, even the forgiveness of sins.' In other words, that's where the power is.

"In addition, let me direct you to Colossians 1:16: 'By him were all things created, that are in heaven, and that are in earth, visible and invisible, whether they be thrones, or dominions, or principalities, or powers: all things were created by him, and for him.'

"You see, Christ created even the fallen Lucifer and his angels, and in reality their very existence depends upon Him who will someday take away from them the element of life and they will be no more.

"Read often verses 9 and 10 of Colossians 2, which tells us that our Lord Jesus is God in the fullest sense of the word, and that we are complete in Him—or in other words, that we lack nothing when it comes to our salvation since He is the head of all principalities and power. The apostle Paul wrote: 'I am persuaded, that neither death, nor life, nor angels [Satan's angels], nor principalities, nor powers, nor things present, nor things to come, nor height, nor depth, nor any other creature, shall be able to separate us from the love of God, which is in Christ Jesus our Lord' (Rom. 8:38, 39).

"Let me add a few words of caution. Have nothing to do with hypnotists, fortunetellers, astrologers, palm readers, and psychics of any kind. Do not associate yourself in any way with professed Christians who converse with demonic spirits when they are 'driven out,' as is done in 'deliverance ministries.' And last, do not affiliate yourself with people who claim to talk with the spirits of the dead. Such people are channels that evil spirits use to break through God's protection around people.

"Again, let me repeat a little of what I said earlier, as it is so vital. If we want power from on high as we pray for ourselves or for others, we must go where the power is to be found. And infinite power is found in the merits of the divine blood of Christ.

"The more we become acquainted with Matthew 27:24-54, the stronger we will become with the enlightenment of the Holy Spirit and Christ's power to save. Also, we need to fortify our minds with the fact that the Holy Spirit is the only means to resist and overcome sin. Only through Him can we live victorious and successful Christian lives. Our prayers will then bring that same great Power into the lives of those we are interceding for (see *The Desire of Ages,* p. 671).

"In this day and age it is vital that we ask our heavenly Father for His Holy Spirit to fight our spiritual battles against self, sin, and the world, and above all against the power of fallen angels. If we pray in this manner for those that we would like to see in the earth made new, we will see the Spirit of God work mighty miracles of redemption in the same degree of those that we read about in Acts 19.

"I suggest that many times throughout the day you should thank our heavenly Father for appropriating to you and your prayer subjects the merits of Christ's blood. If you do this, the Holy Spirit will work in wonderful ways to answer your prayers, and will fight Satan and his spirits. I receive many letters telling how the Spirit of God has transformed lives, remedied desperate conditions, and provided victory for the hopeless.

"Before closing, I want to tell you about an experience that I had more than 45 years ago. Hopefully it will be of encouragement to you. It involves depression. After I accepted Jesus as my Lord and Saviour in 1946, there still came days I would become extremely depressed in my Christian walk. You see, depressing thoughts would fill my mind as I recalled what a God-hater I had been at one time. The fact that I had worshiped Satan and his spirits made me feel terrible. At times it almost convinced me that life wasn't worth living, and that God had no use for me.

"But that hopeless condition always fled when I thought of Jesus in the heavenly sanctuary, and silently said, 'Dear Jesus, please help!' As I see it now, the Holy Spirit would immediately bring to my mind a verse of Scripture that I had memorized, to strengthen me and give me hope. As a spiritist I had learned that demonic spirits delight in flashing thoughts and images in people's minds to activate their imagination, producing discouragement, hopelessness, despair, etc. I understood well what was happening to me.

"Then one day I came across something that excited me greatly: 'Grace is an attribute of God exercised toward *undeserving* human beings. We did not seek for it, but it was sent in search of us. God rejoices to bestow His grace upon us, not because we are worthy, but because we are so utterly unworthy. Our only claim to His mercy is our great need' (*The Ministry of Healing,* p. 161; italics supplied).

"I memorized the passage immediately, and the Spirit of God has used it through the years to encourage and to bring hope into the lives of a great many people.

"Living in this land of the enemy during the closing times of earth's history is no easy task, but we have the assurance that Jesus will see us through it all, and the day will come when we will be recognized as overcomers, and will receive the rewards spoken of by our Saviour Jesus Christ.

" 'To him that overcometh will I give to eat of the tree of life which is in the midst of the paradise of God' (Rev. 2:7).

"I would appreciate if you would let me know from time to time how God is blessing.

"Consider me your dedicated friend in prayer.

"Thank you for sharing your life with me.

"May God bless you in many precious ways."

Peace at Last

According to Mrs. Halstead, who kept me posted on Sharon Lee's progress toward freedom from supernatural oppression, my letter proved to be of great help to her. What I had reminded her about—the strength and grace available through Jesus Christ, and the divine working of the Holy Spirit in her behalf—encouraged her and brought the peace of heaven into her life.

But from time to time the spirits reminded her that they had not forgotten her, and sometime in the fall of that year she wrote to her mother: "Things are going better for me, most of the time. I just wish the spirits would leave me alone all the time. They are such pests, and it seems they never get tired; I wish they would."

Then in December Mrs. Halstead phoned me, saying that evil spirits were again attacking Sharon Lee. The day after Christmas a letter arrived from her, telling about her difficulties. The spirits were again seeking access to her, but every time she prayed to Jesus for help, it came quickly. "When I pray to Jesus for help and protection, I can hear the different high-frequency sounds, and feel as though there is some kind of spiritual battle going on around me. The force is so strong at times that it moves against my body and I feel it in my nerves.

"I believe the Holy Spirit places a barrier between me and the evil spirits, and also drives them away from me. It's wonderful, like some kind of protective force field. Yet I can't figure out why the spirits are still allowed to return, and at times even hurt me. Do you know of any reason for this? If so, please let me know."

Sharon Lee's question had puzzled me in the past as I dealt with a number of individuals who have had similar experiences with supernatural harassment. But after having made the matter a subject of prayer, the Spirit of God led me to see and understand why the spirits boldly intrude into the lives of certain Christians. So I replied to Sharon Lee's important question.

"Dear Friend in Christ:

"It is presently 4:42 in the morning. I have been replying to urgent prayer requests since midnight, and I purposed not to go to bed until I have written to you. I am sorry I did not write before now. The main cause for my delay is that I have been getting so many more telephone calls lately. It seems that distress and perplexity is greater today than even a year ago. The time that I spend with them on the phone is more taxing than before. . . .

"Both you and Deborah have been in my prayers right along, and you will continue to be interceded for according to your needs. Now I would like to reply to a question you placed before me in your last letter: 'Why are the spirits allowed to return, and at times even hurt me?'

"It may interest you to hear that I have been getting a lot of letters telling about supernatural forces oppressing Seventh-day Adventist Christians in various ways. And as I help them to understand that they need daily to plead for the merits of the cross for their salvation, and for the Holy Spirit to fight their spiritual battles, most of them have been able to escape the harassment of evil angels.

"However, in some cases the spirits kept coming back again

and again. Then the Spirit of God led me to discover something very important. As I talked with those individuals about that unique problem, I became aware that they had weak faith in our heavenly Father's perfect plan of salvation. They kept confessing their old sins again and again.

"One woman, named Victoria, said to me, 'Every time that I think about how evil I was before I accepted Jesus as my Lord and Saviour, and about all the wicked things I did, I have a hard time believing that God forgave me all those sins. To make doubly sure that they are forgiven, I confess them to God again. I feel real good after doing that.'

"The thought popped into my mind that the person was in a way actually insulting God every time she did that, adding to her problem. You see, the Bible tells us that we are saved by grace through faith. So if people have a hard time believing that God has forgiven their old sins, I am inclined to believe that their request to have them forgiven again shows a terrible lack of confidence in God, a lack of faith in His Word. First John 1:9 says: 'If we confess our sins, he is faithful and just to forgive us our sins, and to cleanse us from all unrighteousness.'

"I can imagine how delighted demonic spirits must be to cause such individuals to feel unforgiven, then see them ask God to forgive their old sins again. The spirits know that the Bible describes such an individual's unstable state of mind, or lack of faith, as having no value before God in obtaining anything. The Bible says that if we ask anything of God, it has to be in faith, nothing wavering. 'For he that wavereth is like a wave of the sea driven with the wind and tossed. For let not that man think that he shall receive any thing of the Lord' (James 1:6, 7). And I believe that this applies also to the forgiveness of sins. In fact, I believe that such a practice leaves the way open to a great extent for Satan's angels to oppress individuals as often as they wish.

"To help solve the woman's problem, so that demonic spirits would no longer be able to oppress her openly as they had done, I suggested that whenever her old sins presented themselves before her mind, she should immediately thank God in the name of our Lord Jesus for having forgiven all her sins and unrighteousness, and for appropriating to her the merits of Christ's blood.

"I suggested that she memorize Psalm 103:1-4 and 10-14 as a security measure against discouragement. And if any negative thoughts presented themselves before her mind, thoughts that would cause her to doubt God's love for her, she should instantly quote those verses to herself a number of times as a means for the Holy Spirit to stabilize her mind in the power and love of God. There is something infinitely comforting to hear that 'he hath not dealt with us after our sins; nor rewarded us according to our iniquities. For as the heaven is high above the earth, so great is his mercy toward them that fear him. As far as the east is from the west, so far hath he removed our transgressions from us. Like as a father pitieth his children, so the Lord pitieth them that fear him. For he knoweth our frame; he remembereth that we are dust.'

"To cut a long story short, all I need to say is that the woman's new experience has been that many times per day she finds herself praising God for having forgiven all her sins, and for the Holy Spirit successfully fighting her spiritual battles with evil spirits. She says that her Christian walk is now one of peace, contentment, and solid comfort in Christ. And all I can add here is GLORY TO GOD IN THE HIGHEST!

"Sharon Lee, I would like you to be joyful in the Lord and praise Him many times each day for His goodness and grace, and for His Holy Spirit that blesses your life in many ways. This type of living will bring greater measures of divine power into your life and benefit you greatly.

"I should tell you that I wrote a large part of this letter five days ago, as you can see by the date above, and I am now bringing it to a close. So many unexpected things have demanded my immediate attention and created the delay. Your parents have stopped and visited with us this afternoon on their way back from Mexico. They are very nice people.

"Well, it is 2:21 a.m. and I am getting tired, so I will close for now.

A RED SEA EXPERIENCE

"May the peace of God that passeth all understanding bless your life in Christ Jesus."

Let me tell you a little bit more about the experience of the woman I named Victoria. She told of having memorized two hymns, hymns that her mother had cherished and sang often when she was a little girl.

"No longer do I allow depressing and discouraging thoughts to linger in my mind," she wrote. "At their first appearance I start singing or humming those hymns, and praising my heavenly Father for His never-failing grace and love. Mr. Morneau, by the grace of God I have become an overcomer, and I like to think that I am a champion of faith and that my life is filled with spiritual strength that I never had before and never thought possible to receive. I rejoice in saying that I am filled with the sweet peace of God's love."

A DECISION IS MADE

During December 1995 and January 1996 an unusual amount of letters arrived from various parts of the world on the same subject: "visitations of angels." Many of God's commandment-keeping people were distressed by some who claimed to be receiving messages from God for the last days. Although brought to them by beautiful angels, many of those messages were not in harmony with the Word of God, and left some people filled with many unanswered questions.

In almost every letter people would ask if I had thought of writing a book on angels that could help them avoid being misled and losing out on eternity. One man quoted 1 John 4:1: "Beloved, believe not every spirit, but try the spirits whether they are of God: because many false prophets are gone out into the world." He felt that because of my past experience with the supernatural world of spirits, and having been rescued by Christ Jesus from eternal ruin, I owed it to God's people to write a book that would show that not all angels are from God.

Even before that time Reginald Robinson, the *Breath of Life* associate speaker who had given a great amount of help to the

Halstead sisters after their incarceration in the fall of 1988, had suggested that I write a book that would alert God's people to the danger of false angels. I thanked him for his suggestion, but did nothing about it. My prayer ministry was the focus of my efforts. But now the thought entered my mind that perhaps our heavenly Father wanted me to take time and write the kind of book that God's Holy Spirit could use to benefit, enlighten, and wake up His people before it was too late.

Bringing the matter before our heavenly Father in prayer, I explained that there was only one way I could write the kind of book that everyone expected of me. I would have to go to Salem, Oregon, and interview the Halstead sisters about their experience with the supernatural. I felt that in order for me to write with authority on such a complex subject, I would have to see them face-to-face and ask them some hard questions. But in order for that to happen a certain amount of divine intervention would have to take place. I thoroughly believed in the biblical counsel that "the prudent man looketh well to his going" (Prov. 14:15) to avoid bringing all kinds of difficulties upon one's self. God's guidance had served me well through the years, and I was not about to disregard it.

My first concern, of course, was my damaged heart. For almost 12 years it had kept me a shut-in, except to go to church once or twice a month for a couple hours. According to medical science a large part of my heart died in 1984 and has not regenerated. Yes, I had flown from New York to live in California, but that was no joyride. I had to be pushed in a wheelchair from terminal to terminal, with people staring at me constantly. I was not ready to repeat that experience again. (The experience gave me great compassion for people confined to wheelchairs.)

I felt that if my heavenly Father wanted me to go to Salem, Oregon, I would gladly accept "to be strengthened with might by his Spirit" as He did for the Ephesians (Eph. 3:16). Also, there was the matter of money. My wife and I are living on Social Security and a small pension, and have very little left after taking care of our basic needs. We did not intend to ask anyone to help finance such a trip. Having presented my situation before the

Lord in detail, I didn't want to talk to Him about it again, especially since I had hundreds of people on my prayer list who needed intercession. I felt that they should come first.

On the next day a couple whom we know well visited us, and the subject of a possible trip to Oregon came up. Without money being mentioned, the husband said, "You don't intend to make that 1,500-mile trip with your 11-year-old car, do you?"

"I have no choice," I replied.

"The Lord wouldn't want you to do that," he continued. "It's too risky. You need a new rental car, and I am giving you the first $100 toward it. I will also talk to some of my friends, who may want to invest here. You see, my wife and I couldn't sleep nights if you and Hilda took off on that long trip with your old car."

To our great surprise, within two weeks we received checks and money orders that added up to more cash than the trip did cost us, and with the surplus I was able to buy postage stamps for my prayer ministry. You see, I reply to all letters that come from my readers.

In April Hilda and I took off for Oregon, filled with joy in the Lord. I considered the new strength I was feeling as an indication that the Holy Spirit was answering our prayers. Driving comfortably in a new Buick prompted us to thank God for His love and care many times per day.

HAVING A RED SEA EXPERIENCE

On the second day of our trip we encountered a lot of rain as we traveled over the mountains of Oregon. Driving on an interstate at 65 miles per hour is great when the sun is shining brightly and the sky is perfectly clear. But it is something else to keep up with the flow of traffic when rain pours down heavy and furious. The large logging trucks headed from California to the mills in Oregon would whip past us if we went any slower, and would just about push us off the road as they swept by.

The blast of wind and water was so great that all visibility vanished for about five seconds or so as one of the monster trucks whizzed by. At times I felt that the car tires were about to lose their traction. So we traveled with a prayer in our hearts. Then something wonderful happened.

Silently I began quoting scriptures that inspire faith. Verses of the Bible that told of God's infinite love and grace and spoke of His great power. I love Psalm 105, especially the first five verses:

> "O give thanks unto the Lord; call upon his name: make known his deeds among the people. Sing unto him, sing psalms unto him: talk ye of all his wonderful works.
>
> "Glory ye in his holy name; let the heart of them rejoice that seek the Lord. Seek the Lord, and his strength: seek his face evermore.
>
> "Remember his marvellous works that he hath done; his wonders, and the judgments of his mouth."

Then my mind was drawn to Genesis 1:1-7. It relates how God's Holy Spirit moved upon the face of the waters and controlled them at will. His Holy Spirit had divided the waters at Creation. Would He now hold back the rain so that we could drive safely over those dangerous mountains? It was no more than three or four minutes later that Hilda and I began to see something wonderful taking place.

It stopped raining over the northbound lanes of the interstate, and the pavement became perfectly dry. But torrential rains continued to pound the southbound lanes. It was as if a wall of glass about 50 to 75 feet away was keeping the rain from us. And looking to the right of us, we saw the very same thing taking place. Filled with amazement and delighted at what she saw, Hilda said, "What is this taking place? The clouds above us are kept from raining upon us. Surely this is the hand of God blessing our lives."

I explained about my silent prayer and that God was now giving us an experience that we could share with others to strengthen their trust in God. "How long will this last?" she asked.

I replied that it would continue as long as God saw a need for it.

Hilda had kept track of our progress on our AAA map, so that we knew where we were at all times. She wrote down the time the rain had stopped for us, and for three hours and 10 minutes we praised God for His great power and love, and for His giving us a dry road. As we drove along at 65 miles per hour on dry pavement I could see about 20 cars following us closely, but not one ventured to pass us. Perhaps the Spirit of God impressed them to stay with us.

By 2:00 in the afternoon we were both hungry and decided to stop for something to eat. As soon as we entered the exit lane, rain poured upon us again, and, finding a restaurant, we had to sit in our car like any other mortal until the rain abated some and we could get out without getting soaked. That experience made a profound impression on both of us, and we will always remember those three hours and 10 minutes as our Red Sea experience.

CHAPTER FOUR

AN OVERVIEW

efore launching into greater detail of the experience that eventually brought Sharon Lee Halstead and her sister Deborah to a maximum security prison, I believe it's important to examine the unseen forces that were at work and created the tragic events.

First, I need to say that Satan and his fallen angels are greatly interested in the Seventh-day Adventist Church and its people. As I have recounted previously, in 1946 I heard a spiritist priest tell about a number of things that his spirit guide said Satan and his angels planned to do to the Adventist Church as they seek to reduce it into splinters. But one item that I have not yet mentioned caught my attention in a special way because of the cruelty involved.

"In order to do the most damage," the priest claimed, "angels will take on a human form that will be an exact replica of some living Adventists. They will assume the same build, same facial features, same color of hair and eyes, having the same tone of voice, etc. They will then rob a bank, or do other unlawful deeds, and witnesses will report them as individuals whom they know and happen to be Adventists. The law enforcement authorities will arrest the real persons in their homes and charge them with major crimes." The priest's statement produced a few minutes of exciting discussion and laughter among the spiritists; then the priest said something that I'll never forget.

"Our great master Satan has fantastic plans for the Adventists before the conflict closes. To be an Adventist in those coming times will not be for cowards. It will not be for weaklings."

To avoid creating a panic among my readers, I need to say here that our God can overrule and overthrow any and all of Satan's plans. A number of times I heard the high priest tell of almost unbelievable things that Satan's angels started to do against God's people, but suddenly they became paralyzed and the Creator prevented them from carrying them out.

Evil Angels Materialized in 1995

After joining the Seventh-day Adventist Church in 1946, I became interested in discovering what Ellen White had written about the materialization of demonic spirits. Sure enough, I found some interesting references on the subject. For instance, she wrote: "Satan with his angels, in human form, was present at the cross" (*The Desire of Ages,* pp. 746-749; see also p. 733).

Discussing the closing days of earth's history, she said: "The Lord has made some remarkable revelations regarding the experiences that His people will pass through. . . . I have been shown that evil angels in the form of believers will work in our ranks to bring in a strong spirit of unbelief" (letter 46, 1909; in *Manuscript Releases,* vol. 19, pp. 62, 63).

During 1995 I received letters from some of my readers telling of angels appearing to certain individuals with alleged messages from God. These letters have come from various parts of the world, and the writers wanted answers to their many questions about such beings, whether they were really from God. A number of people were especially excited about a being who called himself the angel Gabriel and was appearing quite often to an 11-year-old boy living in Papua New Guinea. The being claimed to bring him special messages from God that the child was to in turn give to a small group of people who were told that they are God's very special people on earth. The angel declared that the Seventh-day Adventist Church had lost its way, had apostatized, and that God had chosen others to represent Him. In fact, one person brought me a cassette tape made by an American visitor that covered the story in great detail.

Of all the things mentioned in the tape, nothing really interested me until I realized that demonic spirits had materialized to the people. I had no doubt about that; it was clear as the light of day. The spiritist priest had explained it well back in 1946, and now I was hearing its fulfillment on a cassette tape 49 years later. Yes, it was just as he had claimed. Materialized spirits would take on the features of known individuals living in an area who happen to be Adventists. I want to relate one particular incident, and in doing so I will refer to the speaker on that cassette as "Van," since that is a part of his actual name.

As far as I can tell, Van has been affiliated with that small group of individuals for quite a while. They left the Seventh-day Adventist denomination, seem to possess a holier-than-thou attitude, stress salvation by attainments, and have the audacity to refer to the church that I love as "the apostate nominal Adventist Church."

I would have liked to talk to Mr. Van, but couldn't find anyone in the United States who knows him or where he resides. If I could contact him I would let him know that he is unknowingly dealing with supernatural beings.

One morning about 60 men who came in trucks and were armed with knives, axes, and other weapons visited the speaker on the tape and some other church members. "When we talked concerning the necessity of coming out of an apostate church," Van said, "they rose up and started shouting, and cursing, and hollering; then they quieted down for a few moments." Told that a dialogue could not continue with the spirit of Satan present, "they rose up in fury and started shouting, cursing, and hollering, and they came rushing at some of us. They knocked me off my seat and pulled my hair. We began praying with some of the faithful who had come out of the apostate church. Some of the brethren told me later that they were making threats against my life. These, I want to emphasize, were from the apostate nominal Adventist Church. The man who pulled my hair and knocked me off my seat was the stewardship secretary of one of the large Adventist churches in the area. All of the men in that mob were brought there by an apostate Adventist pastor, a Judas."

Such incidents are, I believe, another sign that the great conflict between Christ and Satan will soon end. For me to hear of things taking place today that the spiritist priest talked about decades ago as one of Satan's plans to shatter the Adventist Church is exciting and makes me want to tell as many Sabbathkeepers as possible about what Satan seeks to do to the church.

Since my first book on the power of intercessory prayer came off the press in early 1990, a great number of people troubled by SDA offshoot ministries, reform movements, and other groups have sent me videotapes and all kinds of publications put out by such organizations. They ask for my viewpoint on the various fellowships. As a result, during the past six years I have spent a great many hours viewing videos and prayerfully reading many kinds of materials.

After having done all that, I can say in all honesty that I haven't found a single thing that attracts me to any of those groups. I see nothing that would help my Christian experience or that would glorify my Lord and Saviour Jesus Christ beyond what the Spirit of God is already doing in my life. In fact, the more I have thought, studied, and prayed over the question of those so-called reform movements, the more impressed I have become that the time has arrived for me to relate more of what I heard back in 1946 from the lips of that high priest of a secret society of spirit worshipers. As I have said, the priest described Satan's master plan to fragment the Seventh-day Adventist Church. I have written a personal testimony and sent it to everyone who has asked my opinion of any such ministry (see *When You Need Incredible Answers to Prayer,* pp. 59-61).

Avoid Confusion

Also I would like to bring to your attention a book that I consider a masterpiece in making clear to God's commandment-keeping people where to stand while the present storm of confusion beats upon our church.

I regard Clifford Goldstein's book *The Remnant* as a great investment in maintaining one's sanity and spiritual balance. It's a work that will keep its readers from being drawn into the snares of extremists and fanatics. I wish that every Seventh-day Adventist would acquire this book, then read it with a prayer in their heart that our heavenly Father will "grant you . . . to be strengthened with might by His Spirit . . . that ye might be filled with all the fulness of God" (Eph. 3:16-19).

SATAN HAS REAL FEARS

Some people find it hard to believe that the fallen cherubim fears anyone or anything. But Satan has one thing on his mind that causes him a great deal of concern. When we Christians see the devastation his angels have brought into the lives of some individuals, and take the time to reflect on what led them to the desolation they find themselves in; and when we concern ourselves enough to study Satan's methods of operation, as we will be doing in the coming chapters of this book, I can imagine that he will begin to worry. Also, it may be that a sense of fear grips him at the thought that through the avenue of prayer and the power of God we may in the near future do great damage to his cause through our understanding of how he deals with Christians, especially with Adventists, most of whom consider themselves outside his reach.

On page 516 of *The Great Controversy* we find these words: "There is nothing that the great deceiver fears so much as that we shall become acquainted with his devices."

Lucifer and his spirits are skilled strategists who consider themselves brilliant leaders in the conflict between the forces of good and evil. Well-matured plans and previous success in dealing with human beings have made them feel powerful as they move among us.

You may ask just how successful they are. Putting it in everyday language, they are at times very, very successful. For instance, when it comes to involving Christian people in presumptuous courses of action, Ellen White tells us they score highly. In volume 4 of the *Testimonies for the Church* we read: "Presumption is a common temptation, and as Satan assails men with this, he obtains the victory nine times out of ten" (p. 44).

And when it comes to dealing with people in the world as a whole, Satan's angels have phenomenal success. Permit me to illustrate with a book that has recently been on the New York *Times'* best-seller list for more than 140 weeks. On November 29, 1996, the newspaper *Oregonian* carried an article on it. Here are some excerpts from that article:

"Medford—The latest religious book to crack the best-seller list is written by a southern Oregon author who insists Moses got it wrong. The Ten Commandments are the 'Ten Commitments.'

"Good and evil, right and wrong, don't exist. You can do your own thing because God judges no one. How does Neale Donald Walsch know this? God spoke to him in the middle of the night. Walsch asked Her questions, then scribbled the answer on a yellow legal pad, eventually turning the dialogue into 'Conversations With God.'

"The message: If Walsch can converse with God, you can too.

" 'I think there is an enormous hunger in this country right now for spiritual nourishment,' says Walsch, a college journalism dropout who dabbled in public relations, newspaper editing, and stage directing before hitting it big with this book. 'We are becoming increasingly focused and interested in what I call the larger aspects of life. Anything that addresses itself to that hunger will be literally gobbled up.' "

In another news article on the book *Conversations With God,* the manager of a bookstore commented that often people who have read the book are so consumed by its message that they will come in and buy 10 or 12 additional copies to give out to their friends.

Yes, the author of that book is right on one thing—the world right now has an enormous spiritual hunger. And Satan and his angels are taking advantage of every opportunity they can to fill that great need with their deceptions.

CHAPTER FIVE

VOICES FROM GOD

T he beginning of November 1988 was much like any other November in Oregon. The hot summer months had produced abundant crops, wheat being the most valuable one that year. All had been harvested, and the people looked forward to Thanksgiving.

Then something happened that shocked a lot of people and amazed a great many others. On the morning of November 3 the body of a Newberg man by the name of Mike Lemke was discovered at the place where he worked, the Phoenix Horse Farm.

The next day the McMinnville *News-Register* carried this article:

"A homicide investigation has been launched by the Yamhill County Sheriff's Department . . . of a Newberg man, apparently killed by a gunshot. Identity of the victim was being withheld pending notification of relatives believed to be in the Portland area and/or Washington.

"The body was found by a Newberg Fire Department rescue squad that was called to the Phoenix Horse Farm at 17596 Olds Lane, off Highway 240 about four miles west of Newberg, according to Sheriff Glenn Shipman.

"Detectives from the Sheriff's Department said that a bright-red pickup, a horse trailer, and a horse apparently are missing from the ranch, and the horse stables had been burglarized. These incidents are believed linked to the man's shooting death, an official said.

"Detectives were called in shortly before noon when they were notified by rescue crew personnel who had been dispatched to the scene in the belief that it was a request for medical assistance. The body was discovered in a small trailer house behind the stable at the ranch, the sheriff said.

"An all-points bulletin has been issued for the missing vehicle, listed as a 1988 Chevrolet one-ton pickup with dual rear wheels. License number is NZL274, authorities said. Anyone with information is asked to contact the sheriff's office in McMinnville. . . .

"The only information about the apparently missing horse, believed to have been boarded at the ranch, is that it is brown. . . .

"The victim had been employed as a ranch hand at the horse boarding, sales, and training facility of Craig Porter since about 1979, investigators said."

A Summary

Before examining how the Halstead sisters and the Greenes let themselves be deceived by supernatural forces, I believe that I need to present a quick summary of the murder incident here. After studying more than 1,900 pages of reference material on this case during the past eight months, consisting of police reports, court transcripts, newspaper articles, etc., I believe that the material written by Paul Frasier, deputy district attorney of Josephine County, under the title "Scope of Crime," as relating to Sharon Lee Halstead, says it best and in a concise way. Excerpts from it appear below.

"The defendant in the above entitled matter is Sharon Lee Halstead. She was born November 4, 1952. She is the daughter of Richard and Jodi Halstead.

"The defendant comes from a family in which she is a fourth-generation member of the Seventh-day Adventist Church. Her schooling consisted of attending Seventh-day Adventist schools until she was unable to continue due to lack of finances.

"On April 13, 1979, she married Tex Shively. . . . The defendant has two sons by Mr. Shively. The older, Harry (aka Michael), was born April 1, 1976. The younger, Leo, was born January 25, 1979. . . . The defendant and Mr. Shively were separated in 1981 and divorced in 1984.

"Upon the separation, the defendant moved in with her parents for a short period of time in Newberg, Oregon, and then she had several residences in the Salem/McMinnville area before she subsequently established a residence in McMinnville, Oregon.

"In approximately 1983, Richard and Jodi Halstead moved in with David Greene, Sr., and his wife in Wimer, Oregon. Mr Greene, Sr., and his wife were family friends of the Halsteads dating back to the 1950s, when the Halsteads lived in southern California. David Greene, Sr., had a son, David Greene, Jr., who was married to Lynn Sapienzae. Sharon knew David Greene, Jr., and Lynn through this family friendship.

"While Richard and Jodi Halstead were living with David Greene, Sr., they were introduced to a group of Seventh-day Adventists, who were meeting with a Ms. Jean Ketzner in Canyonville, Oregon; the purpose of this group was to become more 'in tune' with God. In other words, the group sought to hear or see God or His angels. Jodi and Richard Halstead communicated to Sharon and her sister, Deborah, what they were learning in this group. Both sisters expressed interest in what was being discussed and learned.

"In 1983 Sharon came to the belief that Lynn Greene was able to receive the word of God either directly from God or through His angels. Sharon claims that in 1983 Lynn Greene told her that God wanted Sharon and Deborah to move to the Grants Pass area.

"Sharon and Deborah did move to the Grants Pass area. This move was quite sudden and was essentially overnight. Sharon left behind household items such as furniture in McMinnville. These items were subsequently sold by her brother, David Halstead.

"In the same year, Sharon and Deborah came to the belief that Leo, Sharon's younger son, could see and hear God or His angels. In particular, Leo was able to hear and see an angel that was known as Naked Truth. This gift supposedly was confirmed by Lynn Greene, and by John Gentry, who in January of 1985 became Sharon's live-in boyfriend. Sometime between 1984 and 1988 Leo lost this gift. However, Leo regained this gift by August of 1988.

"Deborah left the Grants Pass area in December of 1984. She

moved to Texas and then subsequently returned to the southern California area. In August of 1988 Deborah returned to the Grants Pass area. She initially came to Oregon to assist her sister in a custody battle with Tex Shively. However, Deborah was told by Leo that the angel Naked Truth wanted her to live with her sister in Grants Pass. In September of 1988 Deborah moved from southern California to live with her sister in Grants Pass.

"This belief about communicating with God and His angels and also obeying God and His angels became quite profound in Deborah and Sharon. Subsequent search warrants executed at their residence at 414 SE. I Street, Grants Pass, Josephine County, Oregon, found papers on which were questions concerning all manner of items, including religion, and also questions about everyday activities. These questions had written by them answers that apparently had been received from God or His angels.

"What would occur is that the person who had the question would inquire of the person who had the gift, Leo or someone else, and then that person would inquire of God or His angels and repeat what God or the angel had to say. The response would be written down by the question, and the person would be expected to obey explicitly the response given.

"From September 1988 through November 1988 Leo claimed he had the ability to see if someone was 'totaled.' 'Totaled' means that a person has been overcome by evil spirits or demons. The spirit of that person would no longer exist. The body, now a shell, was filled with evil.

"Leo further claimed that to take items from a 'totaled' person was not stealing or otherwise wrong. Further, taking from the adversary, i.e., the 'totaled' person, was simply reclaiming what the Lord intended for the righteous. The same principle applied to destroying property belonging to 'totaled' people. You would simply destroy the property and not allow the adversary the benefit of the property. Destroying a 'totaled' person was not viewed as being wrong because you were not destroying a human being.

"With these principles in mind, Leo announced in September of 1988 the beginning of what Deborah Halstead referred to as 'combat training.' Leo indicated that they (meaning Deborah, Sharon, Leo, and Harry) should go to stores belonging to 'totaled' people and steal items. The group went to such stores as Bi-Mart, K Mart, Fred Meyer, Payless, Albertson's, Safeway, and Shop-n-Kart, both in Medford and Grants Pass. They stole small items. . . . Failure to follow Leo's commands as received from the angel Naked Truth in these areas would result in the disobedient becoming 'totaled.' Becoming 'totaled' was something that both Sharon and Deborah Halstead feared greatly.

"Sometimes Leo would command that they needed to go back to the same store several times in one day in order to steal. Sharon and Deborah would balk at such a request, but because Leo indicated that they would become 'totaled' they complied with his directions. Leo claimed that God would disguise the Halstead sisters so that they would not be caught while taking from 'totaled' people. The Halstead group was never caught shoplifting. This fact caused Deborah and Sharon to believe what they were doing was God's work because of the great number of times they went out and stole and never were caught.

"Leo also directed that he and his brother Harry should go to 'totaled' persons and slash tires on their automobiles. Sharon and Deborah would drive the two boys to the various locations in Josephine and Jackson counties that Leo directed so that the boys could slash tires. One place they went to slash tires was at Roe Motors in Grants Pass. This was on October 14, 1988. There is a police report on file with the Grants Pass Police Department showing that there were slashed tires at Roe Motors on October 14, 1988.

"While at Roe Motors, Leo apparently cut his leg in the process of either exiting or entering the Halstead vehicle from slashing tires. Hospital records confirm that on October 14, 1988, Leo needed stitches in his leg for a knife wound.

"The Grants Pass Police Department has reports of approximately 10 incidents of tire slashing that have been attributed to the Halstead group.

"In furtherance of this 'combat training,' Leo directed that the group, along with John Gentry, should go to the Riverside

Park and assault 'totaled' people. According to the Grants Pass Police Department records, an assault occurred at Riverside Park in which a Michelle Ann Mitchell was struck on the back of the head with a flashlight. Her companion, Ronald Varner, was also hit in the arm. Subsequent investigation by the Grants Pass Police Department, using photo lineups, has identified Sharon Halstead as the attacker of Michelle Mitchell. Harry Shively has been identified as the attacker of Ronald Varner.

"On approximately October 29, 1988, Leo directed that the group should go to the ranch of Craig Porter, located in Newberg, Oregon. At the ranch resided the owner, Craig Porter, a ranch hand, Marston Lemke, and Michael Halstead, brother of Sharon and Deborah Halstead. Leo claimed that all three were 'totaled.' Leo directed that they must go to the ranch. They drove to the ranch and took a dog on October 29.

"On October 31, 1988, Leo directed that they should return to Newberg and take an all-terrain vehicle from the ranch. On the way to Newberg, while driving through Salem, Leo directed that the group should go to his father's residence, [that of] Tex Shively, and steal a gun. At some inconvenience, because of their location on the freeway, they exited the freeway and went to Tex Shively's home. Deborah and Sharon waited in the car while both boys entered Mr. Shively's residence. Leo stole a .38-caliber handgun. Both boys returned to the car, and the gun was given to Sharon. At that point in time they proceeded to Newberg and . . . stole the ATV. On this trip Leo and Sharon test-fired the handgun.

"Between October 31 and November 2, 1988, ammunition was obtained for the gun. Deborah Halstead has claimed that she stole two boxes of ammunition from GI Joe's in Medford. However, the two boxes of ammunition recovered pursuant to search warrants in this matter show that one box of ammunition came from GI Joe's and that the other came from a Bi-Mart store. . . .

"On November 1, 1988, Sharon rented a storage locker at 3610 Rogue River Highway, Grants Pass, Josephine County, Oregon.

"On November 2, 1988, Leo directed that the group must return to the Newberg ranch and steal other items from the ranch.

They did return to the ranch, and taken from the ranch was approximately $50,000 of items, including a bright-red pickup truck, a horse trailer, a horse, a large amount of tack, and other items taken from Michael Halstead's apartment. The apartment was vandalized and was literally 'trashed' by the boys.

"Apparently Leo further directed that Craig Porter, Michael Halstead, and Marston Lemke were all 'totaled.' He further directed that if any of the three were at the ranch while they removed items, they must be destroyed.

"Leo gave specific instructions on who was to do what at the ranch. While there, Marston Lemke, who was familiar with the group as Michael Halstead's family, approached them. After identifying them as Michael Halstead's family, he returned to his trailer located on the ranch property. After loading up the stolen items, Deborah and Leo left the ranch. Sharon, under Leo's directions, went with Harry to Marston Lemke's trailer and shot him three times with the gun stolen from Tex Shively. . . . Michael Shively stood nearby while Sharon Halstead knocked on the door. Lemke answered. There was a brief conversation. Sharon then shot Lemke in the upper right chest/shoulder with the .38-caliber revolver. As he spun around from this first shot, she shot him again in the side. He then fell to the floor with his upper body on a bed. Sharon then at least partially entered the trailer and fired the fatal shot to the side of the neck. A fourth round was fired as Sharon Halstead slipped while running from the trailer.

"Sharon Halstead and her son Michael Shively then left the area in the Halstead vehicle and met with Deborah Halstead and Leo Shively at a prearranged location. The four then proceeded to return to the Grants Pass area, . . . arriving in the early-morning hours of November 3, 1988. . . . It should be noted that upon stealing the truck from Yamhill County, the Halstead group drove the bright-red truck to numerous locations in Grants Pass and took no effort to conceal it. Leo claimed that God would disguise the truck, or, in other words, change the color and scramble the license plate numbers to avoid detection until the truck could be painted. Arrangements were made by Sharon Halstead to have the truck painted. . . .

"On November 4, 1988, the horse that was stolen from the ranch was boarded at Mary Lowe's horse hotel located in Grants Pass, Oregon. On the same day the group, under the direction of Leo, stole a motorcycle from Grants Pass Suzuki located at 1831 Rogue River Highway. That motorcycle was placed in the storage locker at 3610 Rogue River Highway."

We Would Like to Know

For a number of months as I worked on this book manuscript, many individuals have asked me how in the world two intelligent young persons could be led to kill someone without being on drugs or other mind-altering substances. To help people understand the motivating force in this tragedy, I tell them to take a good look at the experience of the Branch Davidians and their leader David Koresh, who in 1993 brought almost 100 of his people to a fiery death outside of Waco, Texas.

For months after federal agents stormed the heavily armed fortress of the Branch Davidians, criminologists, law enforcement analysts, military experts, sociologists, psychiatrists, behavioral scientists, religion scholars, and many others have devoted great amounts of time to studying that tragedy and the reasons it took place.

Being retired gave me the time to listen to special reports on television and to read in newspapers detailed accounts of the research such experts conducted as they sought to explain how David Koresh could lead so many people to their death in the way he did.

They came up with many conclusions, but to me the best and most accurate reason that I have ever heard to explain Waco did not come from the specialists and experts studying Koresh and his followers, but from the satanist priest I knew back in 1946. For a long time I felt reluctant to tell much about what he said. I never even told my own children that I had been a spiritist until they were grown. But as the years go by and events confirm his words, I find myself in each book repeating more and more of what he told his followers.

He explained how demonic spirits use charismatic individuals to manipulate other people, luring them into various types of bondage. The priest claimed that supernatural beings find their best subjects in the religious world.

Adding that spirits can induce thoughts and images into the human mind in such a way that people believe the thoughts to be their own, he also stated that spirit beings can produce powerful feelings in individuals, and a love of the extreme. "Once a person has reached that point," he argued, "the spirits are able to cripple the intelligence and take total control."

Consider the way David Koresh and his people thought and felt. The Branch Davidians held a position common to all extremist and fanatical groups. They believed strongly that they alone had and understood all truth, and that they alone were God's true followers. They felt that the great zeal they possessed for their cause came from the Holy Spirit Himself. It is sad that many Christians place so much trust in the way they feel and do not realize that Satan and his angels are experts at making people feel good about many things, even cherishing error.

In the 1993 updating of my *A Trip Into the Supernatural* I recounted how the spiritist priest said Satan had led much of the world to conclude that he and his demons do not exist. Satan, he said, introduced new beliefs that nullified the Bible, while at the same time he placed restrictions on the activities of the fallen angels (pp. 46-48). From then on, they would no longer be allowed to play with superstitious people. For instance, for centuries in certain parts of the world demonic spirits had led people to believe that it was bad luck to sleep in a room numbered 13, and made sure that many who did would meet with some misfortune.

The inhabitants of rural districts of northern Europe still stir batter in a clockwise direction even to this day, and housewives firmly believe that to reverse directions will surely bring bad luck. The priest explained to us how things that we laugh about today, such as stirring batter counterclockwise, was serious business 300 years ago when Satan's angels reinforced people's belief by bringing some misfortune into the lives of those who did not respect superstitions held by their elders.

He described also how the spirits at times gave power to certain objects and amazed people as they realized that some supernatural force lurked behind it all. In many instances they actually appeared to people as beautiful angels, and at other times they materialized as human beings. In that way strong beliefs and fears held people in a constant state of uncertainty about life, and in a condition of willing obedience. The spirits greatly enjoyed the whole thing because they love to distress, perplex, and oppress us.

The priest told us how Satan figured that a few generations would have to pass before people would look back upon their ancestors as superstitious because of their ignorance of the world about them. "From that time on," he said, "more and more people would declare that Satan and his angels do not really exist."

FASCINATED WITH NEW LIGHT

The Halstead sisters were victimized, taken advantage of, by demonic spirits, because Satan is now removing the restrictions that have held a vast number of his angels in check for more than 200 years. To understand the implication of this, we explore further something that I alluded to previously.

When during the late 1970s certain evangelical Christians became fascinated with what they referred to as "new light," concepts that they felt had been withheld from Christians for too long, they started to press God for new knowledge and insights. Other individuals became obsessed with the idea that the time was right to ask God to allow them to see and talk with angels that would instruct them in new and better ways of serving Him.

A desire for self-exaltation prompted many of these requests. It gave people an unconscious feeling of superiority and security to think that they could learn hidden things from a supernatural being. That they have direct channels with God. Proving the existence of God, knowing more than others do, can be as addictive as any drug. At the same time it opened the way for Satan's angels to appear to certain persons and claim to have come from heaven itself. Little by little such false angels went about perverting the gospel of Christ. As I saw such a trend taking place in some non-Adventist churches, I wondered how long it would take for demonic spirits to infiltrate the thinking of God's commandment-keeping people in such a way and deceive many of them.

Also during the early 1980s, when some Protestants concluded they were becoming demon-possessed, the spiritual leaders who in reality had set the people up to become demon-possessed lost no time in taking advantage of the situation. They held exorcisms that went on sometimes for most of a day in attempts to remove dozens of demons from a person. The power of fallen angels that Satan himself had held back for more than 200 years again operated openly in the lives of Christians.

As I saw these two avenues of access to Christians swing wide open, so that Satan's angels could appear to people as angels of light, I began looking for and reading all kinds of materials by Seventh-day Adventists who claimed to be receiving new light from God through His angels. At that time I was teaching a large Sabbath school class, and asked my class members to bring me any and all materials written by Seventh-day Adventists who made any reference to receiving new light from God or angels.

And sure enough, before long it started drifting in. I discovered that my Sabbath school members had contacted friends and relatives from many parts of the U.S.A. and Canada, asking them to send any materials they came across advocating new light. For instance, I came to know of certain individuals who are now Adventist exorcists when they were just being initiated into that practice. I became aware of independent individuals who had begun sowing discontent and dissatisfaction among the ranks of Seventh-day Adventists before they had attracted enough of a following for our church leaders to notice them.

Voices From God

Some of the materials that came to me through my Sabbath school members told of individuals being instructed by angels about things that would enrich their Christian walk and help prepare peo-

74

ple for the soon coming of Jesus. People accepted alleged revelations on new ways of understanding and pleasing God, especially when it came through children in their early teens or younger. Many individuals did not hesitate to accept the teachings as coming from God, concluding that it would be totally impossible for young children to have conceived such things in their own minds.

Every so often I would receive material telling of someone having received a message from God through a voice speaking directly above them. One man standing in his driveway thought he received a message from God telling him to prepare to build a temple in Oregon, where the ark of the covenant could be kept until the coming of Christ. God supposedly told a woman that He would be unlocking truths for our time by His angels, and for her to be alert and believe. A 14-year-old girl believed angelic beings transported her to various parts of the world and showed her where important events would soon take place.

An angel often visited an 11-year-old boy and took him to certain parts of the world, including Vatican City, where the angel instructed him on a number of important events that would occur there during the closing of earth's history.

THOUGHT MESSAGES FROM GOD

In 1983 the idea surfaced that the dispensation of the gospel had closed and that a new era had begun known as "the dispensation of the Spirit." Some also referred to it as "the advanced Christian pathway to sanctification." Along with it came the message that God had chosen a new way of communicating with His people—through our thoughts. Here are a couple excerpts from material advocating it:

"This communication or speaking through thought *is the basic way* used by the Father to communicate with His people today. This communication network is the very foundation necessary for the reception of the Spirit. It is so important that without this becoming experiential reality in the life, there cannot, and will not, be any connection or relationship with heaven established. This is the very essence of the sanctification process in the life.

"Experience has shown that the main vehicle used in these times is thought, which a believer soon learns to recognize as coming from the Spirit. These thoughts seem like your own, but you begin to realize that on your own, you would not be thinking that way. Moreover, the light given is recognized as something beyond the mind of man to conceive."

The publication also stated that "months later, the angel of the Christian pathway made a personal appearance to a group on a Sabbath afternoon and shed even more light about what to expect on this pathway." The so-called angel informed them that some will be given miraculous powers as gifts:

"This gift . . . involves the ability to control the elements of nature, such as causing rain to fall, earthquakes, droughts, or whatever the Lord wills for the person to do. These people will also be able to transport themselves from one place to another, raise the dead to life, heal the sick, etc. This has been revealed by the angels of the Lord."

It is said that some of the people involved in these beliefs experience visible contact with supernatural beings, and that they see angels both good and bad, converse with them, and witness unusual miracles. In addition, proponents teach that both good and evil angels have names that denote their function, such as Angel of Comfort, Angel of Doubt, etc. They claim that Jesus has come to some as an angel of knowledge.

Another account tells of foreign persons from places such as China, France, Ireland, and South America who have been supernaturally transported to the United States homes of some Seventh-day Adventists. Angels and Jesus Himself arranged for the meetings. I would consider these incidents to be the materialization of demonic spirits. The people involved in such phenomena claim that some Seventh-day Adventists who are experiencing the latter rain have received the gift of tongues to converse with the visitors. The interviews have lasted from a few minutes to a half hour in length after the foreigner appeared within the room.

Also such individuals teach that total perfection achieved under latter-rain sanctification will make it so that a person will no longer have a need for Christ's righteousness. Such an idea is contrary to the plain, simple, and beautiful teachings of Scripture on how to be saved. In fact, it does away with the Bible as the standard, model, and rule by which we are to fashion our lives as the Spirit of God operates in us to make our characters like that of Christ.

The apostle Paul worried that false teachers might cheat Christians of his day of their eternal reward. To the Corinthians he wrote: "I fear, lest by any means, as the serpent beguiled Eve through his subtilty, so your minds should be corrupted from the simplicity [sincerity] that is in Christ" (2 Cor. 11:3).

His concern for God's people was well founded, and he explained in verses 13 and 14 why he felt the way he did: "For such are false apostles, deceitful workers, transforming themselves into the apostles of Christ. And no marvel; for Satan himself is transformed into an angel of light."

And I say to you, my readers, beware of playing games with angels, as it is a very dangerous thing to do. Grandmother Eve did, and we all landed outside the Garden of Eden, living in misery, all of us walking in one direction—to a grave.

CHAPTER SIX

CURIOSITY AND
FASCINATION DID IT

I've written this book reluctantly, yet knowing it had to be done. My only purpose is to expose a seduction that if allowed to continue will place great numbers of nice people outside the walls of the New Jerusalem after the second resurrection.

My desire is to rescue rather than to condemn. To guide others safely across a marsh of spiritual quicksand, rather than let everyone fare for themselves regardless of the outcome. Please understand clearly that the names mentioned in the following accounts appear not as condemnation, but to provide documentation. All names mentioned are a matter of public record, appearing in newspapers, police reports, court transcripts, etc. I consider this book to be a handbook for spiritual survival for many who believe themselves untouchable by the forces of evil.

As I have alluded to previously, during the early 1980s a new phenomenon began to take place in Adventist circles. The topic fascinated a lot of people and created something new for people to talk about. It was discovered that Seventh-day Adventists could become demon-possessed, and some of our Seventh-day Adventist ministers claimed to have actually talked with real demons as they were being cast out. The whole thing was exciting for a lot of people, and stirred up their curiosity to a fever pitch. And it gave the leaders of our church something new to worry about in their role as "overseers, to feed the church of God, which he hath purchased with his own blood" (Acts 20:28).

During the summer of 1981 Elder J. Reynolds Hoffman presented a series of camp meeting sermons on spiritual warfare for the Keene, Texas, camp meeting. All of his sermons were recorded, cassette tapes were made of them, and people bought them as if they were little hotcakes. Shortly after that, other spiritual leaders joined him as exorcists.

Before long a number of incidents took place that indicated trouble ahead for the Seventh-day Adventist Church if such individuals continued in the way they did. To begin with, they operated in the same manner as the Chicago preacher I mentioned earlier. That individual felt that by forcing demon spirits to identify themselves, and also to have them answer questions presented by the exorcist at the time they were being cast out, one could obtain valuable information about the supernatural that in turn could help them in conducting future exorcisms.

But they made two fundamental mistakes. First, they violated God's command not to consult with "familiar spirits" (Deut. 18:11). In other words, they were not to seek information or advice from evil spirits. And if someone did, they were to be put to death (Lev. 20:26, 27; *The Great Controversy*, p. 556). The God of Israel would not allow lying spirits to deceive them.

The second mistake was to stand before the pulpit at the 11:00 Sabbath service and relate experiences that would actually serve to destroy people's confidence in Christ's power to save. Such Adventist exorcists would recount alleged incidents in which Christians were supposedly possessed with dozens of demons yet were totally unaware of it until they heard the speakers mention symptoms that the listeners were also experiencing in their lives. Adventist exorcists would give the demons names such as Jealousy, Anger, Pride, Fear, Allergy, Headache, and Forgetfulness. These are things that even God's people struggle with. We don't need demons to make us jealous or angry. To say that normal human things are caused by demons will convince many who share those same things to assume that they have demons producing them.

Imagine for a few moments someone experiencing any of those difficulties, perhaps struggling with them for many years. The individual has often prayed about the problem. He or she then comes to church to receive some encouragement and a brighter vision of good things to come, but is instead met with the bad news that demons have been operating in his or her life however they wished. That means the person's prayers to Christ have gone unanswered. Consider how shocking such news would be.

It is sad to say, but when one's confidence in Christ, one's faith in Christ, vanishes, then demon spirits can move in and possess. God saves by grace through faith, and if anything or anyone destroys a person's faith, the way becomes wide open for evil spirits to move in and claim the individual as their possession.

Some of the Adventist church leaders who sensed the danger of such exorcisms lost no time in responding to such ideas. In 1982, the year that the story of my conversion experience from spiritism came off the press, the New York Conference president notified all Seventh-day Adventist churches under his jurisdiction not to allow a certain prominent evangelist or his associates to speak in any of our churches. By that time the exorcists had done quite a lot of work in the northern Pennsylvania area, especially at the Montrose, Pennsylvania, Seventh-day Adventist Church, located just a few miles south of the Seventh-day Adventist church in Vestal, New York. A month or so later the president of the Atlantic Union issued the same order for all churches under his authority.

SATAN'S CAPTIVATING FORCE

As I have said before, many individuals find it impossible to comprehend how two adult women, of sound mind and sober, could have killed two persons, and probably four more if the police had not caught up with them as early as they did. Let's look at this tragedy from another angle.

The spiritist priest I have so often cited made this interesting statement one time: "The great master, Satan, gives his dedicated workers a special unction—an unction of seduction. It is a captivating force that leads astray by inducing spiritual blindness."

If we keep this fact in mind as we examine and study the Halstead sisters' experience with the supernatural world of spirits, we will have no difficulty understanding why certain things happened the way they did, and how Satan motivated people to do almost unbelievable acts.

Cassette tapes did for one exorcist what he could never have done just by speaking in churches. The times were right, and great numbers of people were ready for something that would liven up their lives, without giving any thought to the possibility of their being deceived.

People in Oregon particularly responded to this individual's deliverance ministry. An individual by the name of Jean Ketzner, who became one of his right-hand assistants in that state, was considered by many as a person of great spiritual capacity. According to court documents from one of the Halstead sisters' trial, also reported by the Grants Pass *Daily Courier,* she claimed to have the ability to cast out devils and speak directly to God.

Ketzner was some kind of pioneer in Adventist circles when it came to hearing messages from God. And having heard that a woman in Utah by the name of Pat Ferguson-Johnson was also hearing messages from God in her mind, she lost no time inviting the woman and her husband to visit the Ketzner residence in Canyonville, Oregon.

During the Halstead sisters' trial, law enforcement officers did everything they could to subpoena her into court, but she had left the area and couldn't be located. Many were highly disappointed when she couldn't be found. Excerpts from a 209-page court transcript that I have in my possession mentions the judge excusing Ketzner as a witness, and according to people involved in the court case that I interviewed, the judge issued the order to stop law enforcement authorities from spending any more time pursuing her.

MOTIVATED BY CURIOSITY

"In the summer of 1983," Jodi Halstead told me, "my husband, Richard, and I were at the residence of David Greene, Sr., and his wife, Lois, located in Wimer, Oregon. Dave and Lois are old friends dating back to the years when our children were little and we all lived in southern California.

"As we visited, Dave was telling us of some cassette tapes he had acquired from J. Reynolds Hoffman on the subject of demon possession and deliverance ministry. We couldn't help expressing interest in what he was saying about the tapes. They discussed the supernatural and how some individuals had the capacity to control those beings, and were unafraid of them.

"After having heard a few tapes, Dave asked if we would like to attend a deliverance service, the exorcism of evil spirits from a woman that was scheduled to take place at the residence of Jean Ketzner in Canyonville. Dave added that Jean had become a powerful exorcist since she had been tutored by the leading person active in Adventist circles. We were delighted at the idea. The Ketzners had also lived in southern California at the time that we were there, and our children had played together. Now we were looking forward to meeting them again, and especially to seeing her in action, battling with powerful demonic spirits."

I should mention that I have taken the details of this account from two sources: a letter Jodi Halstead sent me in the fall of 1995, and also from notes I made during a visit to Salem, Oregon, during April of 1996.

As I listened to her story, I concluded even then that a strange curiosity played a big part in their willingness to attend an exorcism. And the fact that the subject had already gone through a previous session and "still had a great number of demons in her," supposedly requiring a second service to extract the most powerful and reluctant ones, served only to heighten their interest.

"So, several days after listening to the exorcist's tapes, we went to Jean's place for that all-important session of exorcism," Jodi Halstead continued. "There were about 10 persons present. We all sat in a circle on the floor of an upstairs bedroom, Bible in hand. Donna [not her real name] was at the center of the circle, lying down with her eyes closed.

"Jean Ketzner officiated, and began by reading a few verses of

Scripture, followed by a prayer that denoted a determination to complete the job she had started sometime back. Other persons read verses from the Bible also and prayed; then we sang songs and prayed some more. Jean prayed again, and placed some anointing oil on Donna's forehead, and, having done this, commanded in the name of Christ for the demons to manifest themselves.

"During all this time Donna had her eyes closed, but her body would move some, and her facial expressions kept changing as the demons manifested themselves. Again Jean commanded them to state who they were, and what they'd been doing to Donna. The spirits used the woman's voice box to communicate. Some were very loud and gruff, and produced weird feelings in us. Others were very soft-spoken. Some of the spirits refused to come out, so Jean would say, 'Let's sing "Power in the Blood."' Then the demons would howl, 'No "Blood!" No "Blood!"' They would also cry out in great despair when Jean would place more anointing oil on Donna's forehead.

"Jean conversed with one of the devils who told her that Donna was full of them. Among the many things they talked about, one of them said that he uses television to keep Adventists busy so they will not have time for Bible study and prayer. Some of the demons gave their names, but others did not want to. Here are some of them: Headache, Sad, Weepy, Illness, Pride, etc. The name of one demon was Itch, and as he talked Donna started scratching her arms. The session lasted about three hours, and it left almost everyone present emotionally and physically drained."

While a great number of these séances with spirits have seemed to be successful, some of them have escalated to violence, according to the many letters I have received on this subject during the past seven years from people who have had or are still having problems with spirits. Some writers have told of spirits who were not intimidated by the exorcist, and refused to play games with them. These spirit beings were determined to hold on to their captives at all cost. When the exorcists commanded them in the name of Jesus, the spirits laughed at them and even attacked them physically. Every time I hear of such experiences, it reminds me of the Jewish exorcists mentioned in Acts 19:13-16, who used the name of Jesus as an added tool to their profession. Powerful spirits attacked the men, and they almost lost their lives.

A man by the name of John Gentry, a longtime member of the group I am writing about, was interviewed November 7, 1988, by Sergeant Verlin David of the Grants Pass Police Division, and Larry Pedersbeck from the Yamhill County Sheriff's Department. Gentry told of the danger involved in dealing with spirits who would fight back if need be. Here is a short but interesting part of that interview.

"Verlin David: Have you had very much experience with this satanic type?

"John Gentry: About three years ago I went to some meetings. And they were gonna take devils out of people.

"VD: Where is this at?

"JG: Canyonville.

"VD: Canyonville?

"JG: And, uh, I went there just for the ride to see what would happen. And the people that they were taking demons out of, they reminded me of drug addicts, they kind of acted wrong. And they started acting real spooky. . . . They actually became dangerous . . . and would become violent."

Jodi explained how Jean Ketzner's residence became a center in 1983 for both the deliverance ministry and the gift of hearing and seeing God and angels. On weekends a lot of people convened at her place, especially after Pat Ferguson-Johnson had conducted a seminar on the principles of hearing and seeing angels. Some of the people came from as far north as Eugene to study and pray. Many of them were individuals who believed that they had been delivered from demon possession.

During one of the meetings someone commented that Jean's German shepherd looked so mean and dangerous that he could see why she had him in a cage. Lynn Greene stated that the dog was possessed with a demon of meanness and would bite people, so they kept him in his cage during meetings. Mrs. Greene also mentioned that she had a cat possessed with a demon of "old age." She said that she had talked to God about it, and that He had said that if she were to put the cat to sleep, the demon would have to die with it. But she was attached to the cat and could not see herself destroying the animal.

An Ellie Fitzsemmons supposedly received the gift of healing animals. "One time while a meeting was being held at Dave Greene's home," Jodi Halstead commented to me, "my cat was dying, apparently from poisoning. He was frothing at the mouth, his eyes were rolling back, his gums were white, and he was listless. We brought him to Ellie and asked her to heal the animal. She placed one of her hands on his head and prayed. The cat was healed instantly."

THE SUMMER OF 1983

Great excitement filled the group as for two weeks Pat Ferguson-Johnson lectured on "new light" and how to obtain the fitness needed to receive the gift of hearing and seeing God and angels. She gave every believer attending the meetings a copy of a syllabus that she claimed God had given her. After her departure, meetings continued in the home of David Greene, Sr. People traveled from Boulder City, Wimer, Canyonville, Roseburg, and Eugene. Lynn and Dave Greene, Jr., came from Grants Pass. The various individuals would meet there on Saturday and bring food to share. It was at these meetings that Lynn Greene first started giving messages to the whole group.

Lynn was the first one in the group to hear and see angels, and had prayed diligently for three months that God would give her that special gift. Although other individuals did claim to receive the gift, she became the prime messenger and the central figure in the group. Its members began to depend upon her for answers to the many questions that perplexed their lives. As the meetings continued it gradually became a closed body, with a secret body of information they felt should not be shared with outsiders. "They are not ready for it," said one who could "hear and see."

In October 1983 Lynn Greene said that an angel of God had informed her that the world would end early the next year. She advised members of the group to assemble in Grants Pass and prepare for the great event. As the time for the predicted event came and went she explained the failure as a test of faith. Despite the fact that the failure of the world to end had brought disappointment to many, it wasn't long before they got over it.

Excitement spread among the group as beautiful angels kept appearing to a number of them with great news of good things to come in the near future. For instance, a messenger angel declared that the sealing of the 144,000 was almost finished. A great time of trouble would soon begin as earthquakes and almost unbelievable disasters were about to take place and follow one another in quick succession and increased intensity until Christ returned. The being predicted great confusion in the currency exchanges. Also, that the American dollar would be greatly devalued, and that all those events would happen by April 7, 1985.

The members of the group were led to believe that as the time of trouble would intensify, things would get better for them personally as God used them in greater ways to close His work in the earth. A strange fascination, a captivating force, a devilish attraction was ensnaring them, and few could resist it.

CHAPTER SEVEN

CRIPPLED BY EXTREMISM AND FANATICISM

When a person has moved away from a "Thus saith the Lord" and allows people, angels, or strong feelings to control his or her life and yet at the same time is aware that much of the teachings presented do not harmonize with the Word of God, that individual's conduct shows clearly that the person has left being under the banner of the great Redeemer Jesus and is marching with the deceived. These individuals will find themselves huddled below the walls of the New Jerusalem after the second resurrection.

Such a person may pray to God daily and feel great about his or her Christian experience, but nothing changes the fact that the individual is completely deceived. Someone or something has led him or her to believe things that are not true.

The fact that even good people, some fourth-generation Adventists, were swept off their feet by deception in Oregon should not really surprise us, since Paul's letter to the Galatians documents similar experiences during the early Christian church. As I read the first chapter of his Epistle, I can almost feel his anguish and mental suffering at the thought that probably a large number of people would never recover from their deception and would lose out on eternal life. "I marvel that ye are so soon removed from him that called you into the grace of Christ unto another gospel: which is not another; but there be some that trouble you, and would pervert the gospel of Christ. But though we, or an angel from heaven, preach any other gospel unto you than that which we have preached unto you, let him be accursed. As we said before, so say I now again, If any man preach any other gospel unto you than that ye have received, let him be accursed" (Gal. 1:6-9). Paul makes it very clear to all Christians here that salvation through Christ doesn't come in 20 different ways, but only one— God's appointed way. Also, that our heavenly Father's perfect plan of salvation is as unchangeable as His character: "I am the Lord, I change not" (Mal. 3:6).

The apostle wanted to make perfectly clear not only to the Galatian Christians but to us also that the gospel that he preached along with the other apostles was not some kind of human invention that could be improved upon as time went on, but a God-ordained never-changing solution to the sin problem. In a few words he tells us how Jesus instructed him: "I certify you, brethren, that the gospel which was preached of me is not after man. For I neither received it of man, neither was I taught it, but by the revelation of Jesus Christ" (Gal. 1:11, 12; see also verses 15-19).

QUESTIONS THAT NEED ANSWERS

In April 1996, as I conversed with Sharon Lee and Deborah Halstead at the women's prison in Salem, Oregon, they presented me with a number of questions that they had been seeking answers to. One of them stood out above all others. But being short on time, I promised them that I would answer it in this book. Here is the question: "What in the world happened to us that kept us from seeing how greatly deceived we were, and why didn't God do something to alert us to the great danger we were in? After all, we prayed to Him daily."

It is a two-part question, and I would like to respond to the last part first. It is important for us to keep in mind at all times that when God endowed our first parents with freedom of choice, He also gave them the assurance that whatever the choice they would make, He would always respect it, and would never interfere, even if they made wrong decisions. "God desires from all His creatures the service of love—homage that springs from an intelligent appreciation of His character. He takes no pleasure in a forced allegiance, and to all He grants freedom of will, that they may render Him voluntary service" (*The Great Controversy*, p. 493).

CRIPPLED BY EXTREMISM AND FANATICISM

Our lives consist of choices and decisions. From the time that we wake up in the morning until we go to bed at night we constantly face choices and have to make decisions: the clothes we will wear that day, the amount of time we will give to a particular project, the people we will associate with, and finally setting the alarm clock and the time to get up on the next day. And when it comes to living Christian lives, I thank God for the Bible, His Holy Word, which gives us the guidance we need to make right decisions.

Now regarding the first part of that question: "What in the world happened to us that kept us from seeing how greatly deceived we were . . . ?"

To begin with, the leaders of that group of people studying "new light" had fallen under the control of powerful spirits who made them feel genuinely honest in their conduct and in their religious convictions, thus enabling them to exert the type of influence that allowed them to lead their people into extremism and fanaticism. It is an established fact in human behavior that extremism and fanaticism cripple the intelligence. I look at this as a form of intoxication, numbing and desensitizing the mind. In other words, people in that state have little or no power to understand the horrifying results that following a particular course of action will produce.

To keep their people in darkness, and to avoid them being awakened to their dangerous conduct, the leaders told them not to talk to any minister of the gospel about their "new light," and to keep the supposed messages from God to themselves. Sadly it happened to the Halstead sisters.

ACCEPTING ERROR READILY

Once they have crippled a person's intelligence, demonic spirits can then present even great errors that their victims will then accept with delight. In Paul's Second Letter to the Thessalonians he talks about the "mystery of iniquity" being kept in operation by "the workings of Satan with all power and signs and lying wonders."

The reader may ask how that applies to us today. Every time

that a beautiful angel appeared to Lynn Greene during that period of almost five years, announcing the soon arrival of Christ who would bless His very special people—their little group—a majestic being arrived and declared himself to be Jesus their Redeemer. I consider the whole thing a "lying wonder."

The apostle talked also about "them that perish, because they received not the love of the truth, that they might be saved." He made it clear that God will allow strong delusions to overwhelm such persons so that they will continue to "believe a lie." (To get the whole picture, read 2 Thessalonians 2:7-12.)

Now think for a moment of how much greater and terrible a condemnation will come to those who have given up the love of the truth that they might carry on a relationship with angels who have convinced them that human beings possess a living spirit as well as a physical body. Also, that one's spirit can leave the body and travel to heaven and other worlds, then return to one's body.

John Gentry, a member of the "new light" study group, had a motorcycle accident and almost died. While in the hospital emergency room he had an out-of-body experience. His spirit supposedly went to heaven to be with Jesus. As he looked down from heaven with Jesus, observing the doctors trying to save him from complete death, Jesus asked him if he wanted to remain in heaven with Him or return to earth and do God's will by telling people how to live for God. John told Jesus of his being happy in heaven, but chose to go back into his body on earth to prepare others for Jesus' soon coming.

The most interesting part of this is that John Gentry at the time was an active Seventh-day Adventist. John claimed to have had numerous out-of-body experiences in which an angel would take his spirit out of his body and conduct him on a spiritual trip to heaven, visit other planets, then return to earth where the angel would restore his spirit, or immortal soul, to his body to continue living as a normal human being.

I consider John and the other members of the study group to have been participating in sorcery through accepting errors the Scriptures describe as abominations, such as the supposed immortal soul. The Bible makes it clear that individuals involved in sorcery will perish in a lake of fire (Rev. 21:8).

John once told his group of believers about a particularly horrifying out-of-body experience. An angel supposedly took him to what is known in "their" supernatural world of spirits as "the pit." It is supposed to be a holding place that God has for demons whom He has sent there for special reasons, and those also who have been condemned there by exorcists who have committed them to the pit during exorcism services.

The being conducted John to the mouth of the pit and allowed him to look in. He saw ugly demons fighting among themselves. They attacked each other with foul language and chain saws and knives. Appalled at what he saw, he asked the angel to take him somewhere else. The angel transported him to the moon, where he saw all the equipment abandoned there after the American astronauts departed for earth.

On another trip an angel took John to heaven, where he visited his mansion and even saw his crown waiting on a shelf in one of the rooms. It shone with great brilliance, and he found it hard to leave it. After speaking with Jesus, he met Moses and Elijah, who were deeply interested in what we were doing here on earth. "They asked me what all of you were like, and I replied, 'They are the people of God, and I am honored to stand by them'" he told the study group. "Moses was saddened that we would go through coming trials, for he knew the pain of tribulation; then his sadness turned to joy, for he realized that soon he would meet you all."

John also talked excitedly about seeing the tree of life and was impressed with the size of the 12 gates of the New Jerusalem and the splendor of the whole place.

However, the Word of God warns us that John's experiences were not what he thought they were, because neither John nor any other human being possesses an immortal soul, often referred to as one's spirit. The Bible makes it very clear that humans are totally mortal, and that God only has inherent immortality, "dwelling in the light which no man can approach unto" (1 Tim. 6:16).

What most likely happened was that one of Satan's fallen angels who at one time enjoyed the experience of living in heaven and remembers the beauty and glory of the place put John's mind into a trance, or deep sleep, and by moving upon his imagination in a special way induced in John's mind the entire experience.

As I have mentioned elsewhere, I heard a spiritist priest explain many years ago how evil angels can influence human beings who willingly submit their minds to a hypnotist or any person involved in sorcery. He defined sorcery as "the use of power gained from the assistance or control of demon spirits." Then he explained that acquiring knowledge through the assistance or control of demon spirits is in reality a form of sorcery, whether it be seeking to know what the future holds, or what has taken place in ages past but was not recorded in human records.

"All of us really admired the way John could see the angels with his eyes open, the way people see things in everyday life," Sharon Lee Halstead told me. "We all felt as though John was really favored of heaven and used by the Lord and given more spiritual grace and important things to do, such as trips, messages, etc., because he was a great warrior for the Lord. He was also told that he would go through more hardships for the Lord than any other person on earth had ever gone through before.

"We looked up to John and always wanted to know what God had told him, or where he had gone on his latest out-of-body experience. He was always excited to share these experiences with us. Often we saw John staring up or out into space, and when we would ask him what he was seeing, he would tell of some of the activities angels were carrying on. Those days were so very exciting for us all, just to think that we were admired by God, and considered as His very special people in this part of the world."

Notice how these types of experiences appeal to the sense of being special and belonging to an exclusive group. God wants us to feel special because we belong to Him, not to some human group. All people are special to Him.

INTELLIGENCE BEING CRIPPLED

As Hilda and I spent two days visiting with Sharon and her

sister Deborah at the women's prison in Salem, Oregon, and discussed with them the events that took place in their lives from the summer of 1983 until November of 1988, when the "supposed" angels of God withdrew their mysterious protection from them, I was surprised at their willingness to answer some of the difficult questions I presented before them. To this day I greatly admire the way they have cooperated in helping me write this book, so that others may escape similar deceptions.

"In 1983," Sharon said, "I joined a Bible study group in which I became totally involved and believed in. A while later I was told by Lynn Greene that she had received a message from God for me. She said that God had taken my husband's spirit, removed it from his body, and transported it to heaven. Since God had removed the spirit from the body, demons had totally inhabited Tex, and were using his body. Lynn ordered me to divorce my husband and stay away from him, and not allow the children near him. She assured me that this was God's will, so I did it."

Notice how Lynn Greene's statements go against the Word of God. The human spirit (the breath of life) cannot leave the body, because it is an indivisible unit. If the breath of life is gone, the body is dead.

"I received many such messages from the fall of 1983 to February of 1985. I began to depend on Lynn for spiritual guidance. Three other individuals in the group could 'see and hear' God and angels speaking to them. All of them could explain in great detail what they were seeing. Lynn confirmed that my son was indeed 'seeing and hearing' from God and angels, and that it was a gift from God."

As I conversed with Sharon and Deborah, I understood clearly how imperceptibly they had been drawn into what they thought was a new way of serving God. Messages kept arriving through beautiful heavenly beings who kept telling them that God would soon be using them to accomplish great wonders in the earth. Excited at the thought of doing a great work for God, they were willing to give up everything they owned if need be.

"In October of 1983 I was given a message by my friend

Lynn," Sharon said, "that Jesus was returning to this earth real soon, and that we all had to be ready. I was living in McMinnville at the time in a new two-bedroom house with new furniture and everything I needed. My two sons and I were very happy living there. The message stated that the Lord wanted me to move to Wimer, and to take only what I could fit in my car, such as clothes, food, and my three cats.

"Deborah took my boys down first, and left them with my parents. When she returned, we packed the car, loading it as full as it had ever been. I left all my furniture and everything else that wouldn't fit in the car. My brother David and his wife came and stayed in my house and sold everything they could."

Sharon had told God that she would do anything for Him. Well, she had a big surprise awaiting her. A being brought Lynn the message that God wanted Sharon to give her car away, the only thing of value that she owned. At first it highly distressed Sharon when she got the news, but after thinking about it for a while, she concluded that God would reward her greatly for obeying His command, and she did give her car away.

Can you imagine what that young person must have felt like when told that she must give away her automobile? She couldn't get any money for it, as the command was quite clear—she must give it away. We can see here how demon spirits were trying to have people consider God a tyrant. According to many letters that I receive from people who are having problems with spirits, I see how they love to annoy certain individuals, disturb them, trouble them, and upset them in every way they can, and they do not give up easily. They are relentless in their activities, are cold, cruel, and merciless.

"Early in 1984," Sharon remembered, "Dave and Lynn Greene told us our friend Ron B. and my husband [Tex Shively] were totally controlled by demons. Lynn said that when she looked spiritually at either of them, she could see their eyes as blood red in color. The demons were looking back through their human eyes."

As you can see here, evil angels made every possible effort to get them to accept a number of small errors as a means of preparing them for greater fallacies later. And the sad thing about it all is that things went exactly the way the spirits had planned. Terrible distress and misery shattered the lives of many persons.

"One particular day," Sharon said, "we all went to David and Lynn's house for a meeting, and it was then that I met John Gentry for the first time. People were beginning to look up to him as a prophet, in that he was receiving many messages from heaven, and seemed highly favored by Jesus.

"Lynn gave the message in the summer of 1984 that John and I would be good friends and that it was God's will that our very minds be as one, for only in this way could we accomplish His plans for us. God also supposedly told us through Lynn that there would be a great love between us, and only in that great love would we be able to complete what He had commissioned us to do. Otherwise Satan would try to destroy us so the Lord's will would not be done.

"Then on January 12, 1985, another message supposedly came from the Lord through Lynn: 'It has been foretold that my servant Sharon, and my servant John, have great commissions together and will serve the world. They have been told they must become as one, for only in this way can their commissions be foretold. Their minds and their very souls must be as one. I am the God of love; that is what I have been and will be forever.'"

Sharon said that she and John did become good friends, and after a while he suggested that he move into her place so they could be closer yet. That he did, and for three and a half years they shared everything, and by then John had entertained the thought of marrying Sharon, but some difficulties took place unexpectedly that led him to move out.

The fallen angels intended to do everything they did, so as to prepare the group to accept even more powerful delusions whenever the occasion would present itself. Here is one short experience that demonstrates this. Lynn Greene delivered a message that Sharon and John Gentry were to go into Canada and visit a Seventh-day Adventist minister who was supposed to be ready to receive guidance on "new light."

If I recall correctly, the couple arrived at the Canadian border at night. A number of customs booths were open, and cars had lined up for inspection at all of them. Suddenly an additional booth lit up at the far end, and John proceeded to it. The uniformed officer talked with John for a minute or so, then told him to proceed to his destination. As they left, John immediately said to Sharon that as he had spoken with the officer, the man appeared to be transparent. Sharon was also impressed with the officer's appearance.

"As I looked at the officer," she told me, "I thought he looked perfect. Everything about him was just right: his features, his white gloves, and the way he sat at the window and talked to us. He was wearing a cap with his freshly pressed uniform, and the white gloves made him look so dignified. I was highly impressed by the person."

Then her son, Leo, overhearing her comments to John, said to his mother that it was her companion angel, Sam, who had taken on human form. She immediately turned around to look at him again, but the lights were out in the booth, and no one was anywhere around it. That experience served to establish in everyone's mind a good feeling about their Christian walk. After all, hadn't God cared enough about their well-being that He would have His angels reveal it to them in such a manner?

Some of the things that the group accepted were so bizarre that only individuals whose minds had been crippled by extremism and fanaticism could have possibly believed them. For instance, David Greene, Jr., became convinced that he could use an invisible sword to rid his house of evil spirits, and actually took up the practice and demonstrated it to a number of people. The subject came up during Sharon Halstead's sentencing hearing in September 1989 while John Gentry was on the witness stand. He was asked a number of questions, and here is an excerpt from the court transcript:

"Q: Among the people in your group, who were the primary ones who were able to hear?

"A: In the very beginning it would have been me and Lynn

and Denise. And then toward the end the people who could hear were not telling their messages to other people, and the members who couldn't hear or see would ask questions and they would get answers from them.

"Q: Did you ever have occasion to see people fighting evil spirits at the Greenes' house?

"A: I don't understand that.

"Q: Let me go about that another way. Are you aware of an invisible sword?

"A: Yes.

"Q: Could you tell us in your own words what that is?

"A: . . . It's like a spiritual sword, and it would be used to clean the house of any demons. . . .

"Q: Did Dave Greene have an invisible sword, or a spiritual sword, as you describe it?

"A: Yes, I believe so.

"Q: Did you ever see him use that?

"A: Once, but I didn't really believe much to do with it.

"Q: Could you describe as best you can recall what you saw?

"A: He moved around the room slowly with his hand out, as if grasping something. . . .

"Q: Did he tell you what he was doing?

"A: Yes. . . . He mentioned that he had been bothered that day by a lot of things that had gone wrong; they were caused by an evil spirit. Before we had our Bible study he would like to clean the house out because he knew they were around . . ." (Circuit Court of the State of Oregon, transcript of Sharon Lee Halstead's sentence hearing).

Such reasoning naturally perplexed the law enforcement officers as well as the court officials. They had never heard of such a belief, and it took a while for them to get accustomed to the idea. The court also questioned another man by the name of Ken Cook about David Greene, Jr., and his invisible sword. Mr. Cook and his wife, Denise, had been Adventists for less than one year when they were drawn into the "new light" group. They were forced out when they began to question some of the things they noticed. Here are some excerpts from Ken's testimony.

"Q: Would you state your name, please?

"A: Kenneth Cook. . . .

"Q: Where do you live?

"A: 300 Newt Gulch, Wilderville. . . .

"Q: You have been interviewed by the police a few times in this case; is that correct?

"A: That's correct. . . .

"Q: Mr. Gentry's testimony—would you agree pretty much with what he described as far as this group was going when you first got involved?

"A: I would like to clarify a few things, . . . mainly with our involvement in the group. We got involved in the group at . . . the beginning, basically on the deliverance ministry. . . . We were riding the thing out because it was sensational. . . . We had set aside reason and we accepted what we could handle with our hands, and what we could see with our eyes, and hear with our ears, rather than accepting the counsel from the church or other individuals who would be better experienced in these fields.

"Q: Why didn't you talk to someone in the church about this?

"A: Well, I attempted to go to members that I respected when we first had reviewed this material, but I believe it frightened them. We had been in the church less than a year, and we really didn't understand . . . what we were doing. And the reaction of these people seemed [to be] fear, rather than saying OK, we'll sit down and figure out if this is right or wrong. . . .

"Q: Who was actually leading the group when you were first involved?

"A: It's hard to say per se if there was a leader of sorts. I became acquainted with the deliverance ministry through David Greene. . . . I was interested, because my wife was deathly sick with a disease by the name of lupus, and it was said that sometimes these things can be caused by demonic cause. Modern medicine said there was pretty much no hope for her. . . .

"Q: Who else was getting messages in the group when you were involved?

"A: I believe that the deliverance ministry was just evolving into this message ministry. As far as I could see, it was something that was just taking place. There were individuals I had never personally met that were making predictions about things that were going to happen. . . . When I expressed my concern I was told I had a demon of doubt. And when I began to raise objections over certain things, we were forced out at that point.

"Q: I believe you told the police you went and talked to David Greene about it, David Greene, Jr.?

"A: That's right.

"Q: Can you describe that meeting?

"A: I had found some very interesting Bible texts and quotations, that if we would sit down rationally and examine the information and other material, there would be only one conclusion that we could make. . . . I went to the door, and I recall he said come in. Dave Greene invited me in. I sat down. The moment I sat down the phone rang, so he excused himself and picked up the phone. It was a man by the name of Lantis, and David spoke with him and put the phone down, and informed me that 10,000 demons just walked into the house, Lantis just told him that . . . That took away any powers I had. . . . [About] six months had passed since we left the group, and David [had previously] explained to me that they had learned all kinds of new things, and he produced [what he said was] an 'invisible sword,' which he [used to] clean the house out of all these demons.

"Q: Can you describe what he did to clean the house of the demons?

"A: Well, I don't clearly picture what he did anymore, but I remember that he did something that would be hand symbols, and he went about the house with the sword in a symbolic way.

"Q: He didn't actually have a sword in his hand?

"A: No.

"Q: You have been out of this group since that time, I take it?

"A: Absolutely" *(ibid.)*.

CHAPTER EIGHT

CONFUSION UNLIMITED

S atan's angels, parading themselves as the Creators, were pouring out confusion to this group of people, and they accepted it without hesitation. But confusion, like any intoxicant, can cause individuals to become dizzy and lose their sense of direction. And that is exactly what happened to those nice people in Oregon.

A 500-YEAR-OLD MAN

Reading through police reports on this case, I came upon one especially interesting account. It illustrates what a person is willing to believe once he or she starts down the road of listening to deception. David Greene, Jr., had called for a police officer to visit him as he wanted to tell about a 500-year-old man who had been a guest in his house for almost three years. He thought it important to tell the police his side of the story, so that he would not be misunderstood in case someone else had told them about it. Here is a short version of what the police officer wrote down:

"When I arrived at the Greenes' house I spoke with David . . . who said that during the time that this imaginary old man was in his home, Lynn Greene was the only person that could see and communicate with this old man. This old man was named Timothious . . . David said that as time went on he was able to communicate with Timothious also.

"David did explain that Timothious was around for about two or three years; he also explained that while involved with this belief, he would sit in the middle of his living room floor and talk in tongues. . . . David mentioned that when he went on spiritual trips, people that were present would ask him what he had seen.

"David mentioned that John Gentry also was able to do this spiritual traveling. On one occasion Gentry and David both saw the same things while on a spiritual trip."

David Greene, Jr., and Lynn Greene's black notebook contained additional information. Timothious supposedly had lived more than 500 years ago in the Himalayan mountains, where he spent two years in a cave writing "Books of Truth." These books were to stay in the cave until God decided to give them to His people during the time of the end.

Angels claimed to have brought Timothious to stay at the Greene home. The man was supposedly in another dimension that only Lynn could see in. He enjoyed riding in their new car and eating Popsicles out of their freezer. Sleeping or just sitting in a brown lounge chair, his favorite place to be, he liked to watch television, especially *The Price Is Right.*

Timothious would tell David and Lynn Greene about his family, wives, and children. They had turned away from God, and he had long outlived his whole family. God had offered Timothious the choice of either going to heaven right then, but dying first, or staying on this earth, where he would never die and would see Jesus come, but would start aging. During the time that he was with the Greenes, Lynn saw him age some.

This "new light" group had all kinds of excitement in their lives as fallen angels kept visiting with them in response to their prayers. On one particular day while the group were studying together they were told they had the great honor of being visited by the 24 elders from around God's throne. And one additional surprise was that Queen Esther of the Bible was also with them. Lynn, John, and Cheryl could see and converse with them. Cheryl asked Esther about the gold ring she had on her finger. The "queen" replied that it was a wedding ring given to her by her husband the king.

Some of the angels stayed with David and Lynn for days at a

time. The couple talked to and consulted with them about biblical topics and their daily living. Some of those angels claimed to have interesting and attention-getting names. Here are a few of them I have taken from the 160 names listed in Dave and Lynn's black notebook.

Angel of Truth	Angel of Mystery
Angel of the Morning	Angel of Deliverance
Angel of Gladness	Angel of Energy
Angel of Speed	Angel of Good Health
Angel of Great Strength	Angel of Warmth
Angel of Destruction	Angel of Was, Is, and Is to Be
Angel of Success	Angel of Motherhood
Angel of Tongues	Angel of Beyond the Stars
Angel of Trumpets	Angel of Dusk
Angel of Trees	Angel of Ten Names
Angel of Long Journey	

Besides this, the Greenes believed that they could pray for and receive any angel they wanted to talk with, and that angel would fly down from heaven to answer any questions they asked. Some of the advice the beings gave the Greenes was intended to separate them more and more from the Seventh-day Adventist Church. The beings told them to read and pray at home on Sabbath instead of going to church because the group already knew more than all the other church members, and the preacher was not spiritual enough to feed them.

Would you believe that one angel claimed that Neal Wilson, our General Conference president at the time, was to be "totaled" and an enemy of the church! And listen to their opinion of evangelistic meetings: "They are a waste of time and money."

"There were many times," one of the group said, "when we were together as a group studying that Jesus Himself would come down and answer our questions, instead of an angel answering them. When Jesus would appear in Lynn's home, He came with thousands of angels, and she said that she could see the whole place light up from the brightness of Jesus and the holy angels.

All the angels would be bowing at Jesus' feet while He was talking to us, either giving us a message for the group or answering our questions individually.

"Lynn said Jesus smiled at us all the time and was always happy to come down among His people on earth and spend time visiting with them. Jesus would raise His hands over us and bless us and look up toward heaven and pray to His Father, and ask Him to bless and keep His children safe here on earth. Jesus told us that He knew we would be going through a lot of terrible things with the trials ahead, but that He would protect us from the attacks of the enemy [Satan]."

Angels brought messages from heaven on certain individuals' birthdays that were quite amusing. The members of the group received things that they referred to as spiritual gifts. Things that were kept in heaven for them until their arrival there after Christ's second coming. For instance, in November of 1984 an angel reported that Jesus had given one woman a herd of 77 blue-and-white cows, as He knew how greatly she loved farm animals. The Lord Jesus also gave her three horses with wings, one stallion, and two mares. Also to her great delight the being informed her that soon the mares would have little ones. And to add to her surprise, Elijah had come with the angel, and he gave her a big hug.

MORE CONFUSION

The following is a copy of a letter found among materials the Grants Pass Police Department obtained during the investigation they conducted in their effort to bring out the facts about the "new light" movement, and how its teachings could have led to the killing of two individuals. One of the active members of the movement (referred to at times as one of its leaders) wrote to a friend he was seeking to persuade. Except for name changes, I have reproduced the document as written, including misspelled words.

"Dear Brian,

"You know that I am not much on writing letters, but I have a gift four you. I have learned many things since we last talked.

There is a way to see and hear into the spiritual world I don't remember what I told you a long time ago but I will explain just a little bit.

"When you pray that your mind be clear and open that all evil be behind us the Lord uses your own thoughts to talk to you many people hear but don't know and take it as if they were their own thoughts. The same goes for angels. Sometimes they will stand right beside you and talk to you and you thing that you are talk with your self, but how can you talk to your self when you know what to say.

"Their are two things it can be evil spirits or good angels, it is like turning a radio to high frequency and learning to hold it there for our minds tend to wander very easily so it takes practice progressing in longer and longer periods of time Evil tells you that you are talking to your self and makes you think that but pray for faith to keep listening.

"In the Bible we seem to think that the voice of God was heard audibly all the time but many cases it was transferred by thought it is men's spirit communing with God spirit for this worship in spirit the inner man seeing is also in the same way though one of our friends can see with his eyes the spiritual world we see with spiritual vision it is like a dream in the day time, Pictures is another name it is God using our imagination for He is the one who created it.

"A lot of people have dreams at night because our conscious level cannot get in the way with preconceived ideas doubt or unbelief there for being able to accept it. Nightmares are from evil. From a small description of these gifts we can see and hear angels we have met and talked to many and have made many friends whom we love very much to date 160 [sic] each other has a specific name which also describes there duty. For example Thuth is the angel in charge of truth. Good will and Joy brings and sings a lot Joy. Rain brings rain and what ever else you can thing of. For names there are many.

"There are special Seven angels thoughts. These seven are the seven spirits of God mention in Revelation their names are

Michael, Gabriel, Sarakiel, Raphael, Raguel, Ureil, Phenuel. Under these angels run all the affairs of this universe. For every word in the Bible that deals with the earth and man that is the name of angels 'For my words are Spirit and life.' You have a companion angel to be your companion and friend besides the gardian angel and if you ask for more they will come. Each angel has a personality as varied as us people but all love us very much and if you tell them you love them it makes them very happy and they might even hug you.

"The tape I am sending you is a tape of the music that angels have made to show you that heaven is not the funeral music that your mom used to play on Sabbath 'boring.' Al musicians have the Gift of music says the Angel of music but most of the times they are influenced and used by the evil ones and the music is perverted many times it is just the music that is perverted and not the words or visa-versa. These songs were pick out from what he could get at the time but there is many more we have to wait and find them.

"I will tell you about a few of them the eagle is representative of the angel Phenuel? and if you listen you wil recognize they are singing about angels. The whistler there is an angel called this and if you think that you see happy angel dancing to this song believe it.

"The angel of music rewrote its along way home and logical song but the angels of poetry wrote the words to the logical song so listen to the words and see Jesus talking to us and let your spirit be happy. Each group has a certain percentage of music that is from the Lord some are 2% Rev speedwager? to Abba 45% to Fresh air 98%. So later I can send more if you want.

"Must go now getting sleepy,
"Love Henry"

The writer of the above letter was not under the influence of alcoholic beverages or hard drugs when writing this letter, being totally dedicated to healthful living. Neither is he illiterate, having graduated from college. What we are seeing here is unlimited confusion produced by Satan and his fallen angels. They had messed up his mental faculties by moving upon his imagination and playing with his emotions.

The being created in the person a strong sense of being wise because he had acquired so much "new light" from what he believed to be God's angels. It saddens me every time I see demonic spirits taking advantage of people.

While Satan's angels are experts at deceiving human beings, they do not stop there, but find great pleasure in oppressing people in any way possible. According to letters that I have received from people who have had trouble with the supernatural, they love to annoy people, disturb them, trouble them, and upset them in every way they can, and they do not give up easily. Relentless in their activities, they are cold, cruel, and merciless.

STRANGE WOMAN

"In the summer of 1986," Sharon Lee Halstead reported to me, "David and Lynn told us about the great amount of information they had received from God and His angels regarding an extremely wicked being known as 'Strange Woman.' She is the strongest evil power that can live in and inhabit a person's physical body against one's will. The being can read your mind and know what your every move is going to be. On this point and many others she is more powerful than Satan himself.

"This information served to burden our minds with additional worry as we tried to avoid doing anything that could bring her into one's life. Even at that, John Gentry had an encounter with her that distressed him greatly, even to the point of thinking that he might die.

"In late spring of 1987 he had gone to bed earlier than usual and was curled up on his right side in the fetal position. Suddenly his body started shaking all over, and he didn't understand what was going on. Lying there on top of the blankets, he tried to pray for God to help him. I called David and Lynn as John had asked me to, and they told me it was an attack of the Strange Woman and demons, and that I was to command the demons out and to pray they would not come back.

"David and Lynn were both on the phone with me at the same time. I was scared not knowing what was wrong with John, and they told me that they would pray for us and that God would send extra angels to help battle the demons harassing John. After our phone conversation I saw that John was still shaking. Then he got up and went into the living room and lay down in front of the heater. He remained there for almost two hours. I brought a blanket and covered him up while he prayed for God's help.

"An hour later his body slowed down, and after another hour the shaking stopped completely and he fell asleep. After that John no longer wanted to talk about Strange Woman. Dave had told us that even talking about her would give her the right to trouble us."

Sharon Lee said that the group believed that the supernatural being could read minds. Several Ellen White statements reject this idea. In the little book *Confrontation* (p. 13) she says that Satan knew what Eve was thinking at the forbidden tree only because she was unconsciously talking out loud. Clearly, he could not directly read her thoughts. In *Messages to Young People* (p. 328) and book 1 of *Selected Messages* (p. 122) she clearly states that Satan cannot read our thoughts. Also, how could any evil power be more powerful than Satan himself? Such questions should have cautioned the Greenes' followers, but they did not analyze what they were being told and compare it with inspiration.

CONFUSION AND FEAR

I would like to share a bit more information about this alleged supernatural being. It shows what people can do when motivated by fear, and appears in a court transcript of Deborah Halstead being interviewed under oath.

"Q: Deborah, I want you to talk about a couple of areas. First, about Strange Woman.

"A: OK.

"Q: Mr. Frasier mentioned and asked about Strange Woman.

"A: Yeah.

"Q: Back in the time period we're talking about, let's say September and October of 1988 and early November, when all of these events were taking place, were you informed that Strange Woman and Satan had been put someplace?

"A: Yeah. Leo said that they, let's see, I can't remember if he said that we were supposed to pray about it or what exactly, but we prayed and asked that Sharon be made to learn about the Strange Woman before anyone else. And . . . the whole reason . . . we were having to pop tires and steal and do those things was . . . that Sharon . . . asked to have the knowledge before anyone else, [and] that's what she got, and we started learning about her; and because we had learned about her, then we were being trained in how to fight against her and deal with her. And then at one point we had prayed and asked that she and Satan be sent to the pit, and Leo said that they were bound and gagged and sent to the pit, and that's where they were, and in order to keep them there we had to do these things.

"Q: OK.

"A: Otherwise they would get out and come and kill us.

"Q: So, besides the fear of becoming totaled if you didn't do this, do I understand you that also you felt that you had to do these things to keep Satan and Strange Woman from getting to you?

"A: Yes, from killing us.

"Q: So they had to be kept in the pit?

"A: Yes.

"Q: Now, Mr. Frasier also asked you, Deborah, about how you reacted to the threat of going totaled, and you said, you know . . . Can you describe it a little more graphically what your feeling was at the time? I mean, were you in mortal fear . . . ?

"A: We were in extreme terror, yes.

"Q: Was it more important . . . well, your belief would be that . . . ?

"A: The spirit being more important than the body, yes.

"Q: Yes, that you could give up the mortal body, but if you lost your soul it was forever?

"A: Right.

"Q: Would you, Deborah, also . . . and it's difficult to do on a printed record, but when you say that Leo would be talking to an angel, would he be looking someplace?

"A: Yes, he would be looking up.

"Q: Just as I'm looking up at Mr. Frasier here?

"A: [Ms. Halstead nods head affirmatively.]" (court transcript of Josephine County and Yamhill County).

The group was living under terrible bondage. Demonic spirits had robbed them of the peace of God's love, had crippled their intelligence, and kept them thinking continually about all the evil that could overwhelm them. They had lost sight of our great Redeemer, Jesus, and His power to defeat His enemies no matter what they did.

To help us understand some of the pressures they found themselves under, consider some things Sharon said during our prison interview:

"In October of 1988 my sister Deborah, my boys, and I were driving to Medford on another mission given us by an angel. As I was driving I felt angry at how God's angels were always rushing us on to another mission, with barely any rest in between. I wanted to do the Lord's will, and to do His will meant obeying immediately when given a mission. An angel told us that this would please Him greatly.

"I hated being rushed around, but felt driven to complete a mission out of fear of offending God and being lost. For a few miles I had a very strong urge to plow my car into the rear end of a semi I was following. I could not understand why we were having to drive so much in doing things for God. I was tired and very stressed at doing them. I wanted to just ram my car into the back end of that big truck and end it all. The tremendous urge to do that went on for several miles, then I decided not to do it, because I really wanted heaven, and knew that if I were to destroy myself I wouldn't reach it and neither would my children and sister. Today, I know and understand why our heavenly Father didn't allow me to destroy myself."

Another time Sharon described how she felt when told by an angel to go to a certain store and steal things—how she hated doing it.

"These crimes were never planned or premeditated, but at the spur of a moment, acted upon the directions given to Leo by an angel. Having never stolen anything in my life, I hated doing it, but had been told it was a test of my faith and loyalty to God. And if I did not obey God's directions, He would remove my spirit from my body and I would be totaled too. Because if I was not following God, then I was following Satan.

"Then one day an angel told Leo that the Greenes' son had chosen not to follow God and that the parents, because of their love for their son, had followed him and also become totaled. That God had taken their spirits to heaven and they were looking down upon us and wanted us to destroy their physical bodies so the demons could not possess and control them to use to hurt God's people. I began to worry, and dreaded the day we would be told by an angel to destroy them.

"It was not our duty to destroy the bodies of all who were totaled. For instance, we were told that almost all of the police department and Grants Pass residents were totaled, but we were to kill only those we were specifically told to destroy."

As we have seen, confusion and fear can lead people to do some strange and horrible things.

CHAPTER NINE

A TRANSFER OF POWER

For a period of five years Lynn Greene acted as a prophet for the little group of some 20 persons. While a few others apparently could see and hear in their minds what they believed to be God and angels and received many messages regarding their own lives, Lynn's commission (supposedly from God) was to nurture her little band of followers with divine guidance.

Then in the summer of 1988 a transfer of power began when the alleged Angel of Motherhood informed Lynn that before long her prophetic role would put too many demands upon her. Because of her pregnancy God was relieving her of the great responsibilities she had been carrying for His cause. The being said that God would remove from her the gift of "seeing and hearing" and would pass it on to another person in their group.

This announcement was a big surprise for Lynn, but she accepted it without showing any disappointment. At the end of June 1988 Leo Shively, younger son of Sharon Lee Halstead, began claiming to be receiving messages from God and His angels. The child was 9 at the time.

"We were lying on my bed," Sharon said to me, "when I noticed Leo staring at several places in the room and just staring. I asked him what he was looking at, but he didn't answer at first, so I asked him again, and his mind seemed to be absorbed in something out of this world. Then gazing intensely at him, I asked, 'Are you seeing angels?'

"He replied that he was, adding, 'One angel is real big. He goes way up above the roof of the house.'

"A few days later," Sharon continued, "after Leo started seeing and hearing, I called Lynn and asked her about how she saw Jesus and the angels. She replied that when she saw Jesus, He was very bright. Sometimes she saw great brightness radiating through the holes in His hands, feet, and side. I told her that was the way Leo saw Him also. Lynn added that she had been told that Leo's spiritual sight was so good that he could see angels and demons 20 miles away.

"As I talked with Lynn, she stated that her ability to see and hear the supernatural had reduced greatly. All she could see was her Angel of Motherhood, the hedge of angels around their home, and Timothious, the 500-year-old man that supposedly lived with them at the time."

An interesting little bit of information caught my attention as I talked with Sharon about those days. "Everywhere we went," she said, "the angels that Leo could see went with us. These were some of the angels that we had talked to with Lynn at her home. They were bright and beautiful." Then she told me about Leo having a frightening experience.

"Leo and I were lying on my bed one day in July. I was trying to get him to take a nap. While we were resting there the bed started to shake enough to scare us. We really felt tossed about after 10 or 15 seconds. Leo looked under the bed and then grabbed my arm very tight and wouldn't let go. 'It is an ugly demon shaking the bed,' he announced. The child was extremely frightened. I asked one of our accompanying angels to destroy the demon that bothered us, and he did. The bed never shook after that."

ANGELS OF OPPRESSION

For about five years the supernatural beings claiming to be from the throne of God charmed this small group of people with promises of wonderful things to come, winning their confidence and love. Then suddenly a new order of things began. The beings evicted Lynn from her leadership responsibilities and ended her role as a prophet. Alleged angels now visiting a 9-year-old boy informed him that God had chosen him for a very special role in these difficult times.

Angels would help him, but God expected him to act as a

valiant young man, showing himself to be brave for the service of God when difficult situations confronted him. The supernatural beings instructed him never to doubt the words of a messenger angel, even if what God asked him to do seemed to contradict what he had been taught to be right. The next few months, he was told, were crucial to the closing of God's work on earth.

Those magnificent beings then began to lead Leo Shively; his mother, Sharon; his aunt Deborah; and his brother, Harry, into activities forbidden in the Word of God. Under the pretense of getting things ready to help great numbers of Sabbath observers with money and other things they would need during the time of trouble, the angels informed them that since God owned our planet and everything on it, they should not be surprised if He asked them to store things for Him in certain places. The supernatural beings told them clearly that God wanted them to begin transferring objects that belonged to "totaled" individuals to places where they would be kept for the time of trouble.

As we mentioned earlier, the Halstead sisters and the others were instructed to go to certain stores and carry various objects out, and no one would see the merchandise, as the angels would make the objects invisible. Nor would anyone stop them. And sure enough, the little group did the most unbelievable things with the help of supernatural beings. It convinced them beyond the shadow of a doubt that they were completely under the care of God's angels. What a terrible shock they experienced a few months later when Satan's angels double-crossed them. Arrested, the two sisters found themselves incarcerated.

One thing that especially caught my attention as I studied the case during the writing of this book was the great amount of pressure the angels exerted upon them to shoplift and slash tires. Some days they worked from early morning until late at night without having any time to rest, and came home totally exhausted. Here is an excerpt from a court transcript in which Deborah was interrogated.

"Q: You made mention, but I'd like you to tell a little more about when Leo told you that you had to go out and steal things, and when he told you that you had to destroy totaled people. Did you and your sister Sharon argue with him about that?

"A: Yeah. We didn't want to do it. He said that we had to, or that we would go totaled, that we didn't have any choice.

"Q: And you believed that, didn't you?

"A: Well, sure. Because he got all upset and would cry and carry on, you know, and he came over and hugged us and kept crying and saying, 'I don't want you to go totaled; you have to'; . . . 'You have to do these things so that you don't.'

"Q: And so you'd go do it?

"A. Right.

"Q: Now, you've described a period of time where apparently you were doing a lot of shoplifting?

"A: Yeah.

"Q: I mean, were there whole days, Deborah, when you did nothing except go from store to store?

"A: Mm-hmm, and that would be from early morning until the evening.

"Q: Would you be tired?

"A: I mean, early morning from when the stores first opened. Yes, extremely.

"Q: You've mentioned some of the stores. Did you ever take anything in Grants Pass from Safeway?

"A: Sure.

"Q: And I—well, did you go back into the same stores again and again?

"A: Sure.

"Q: And do I understand what you're describing as in comes Deborah Halstead, Sharon Halstead, Harry and Leo Shively, and you go around and take a bunch of things and then leave without reportedly buying anything?

"A: Yeah.

"Q: And no one ever said a word?

"A: No.

"Q: And would it be fair to say that this made you even more

114

convinced that Leo was in fact talking to an angel?

"A: Of course.

"Q: Now, Deborah, did Leo ever have you take anything from the [animal shelter]?

"A: Yeah, he had us take a pit bull down in Medford" (Crago & Associates court reporters, vol. 2).

The pit bull incident is interesting when you consider that a penned-up pit bull isn't the easiest thing to steal, especially when other dogs are in adjoining pens ready to bark aggressively. The angel had promised that the venture would be a success, in that it would be done in total silence. Kennel door 9 would be unlocked, and all they had to do was to bring a certain size collar and leash and walk the dog away. And to their amazement and delight, they accomplished their mission in perfect silence, with every dog in the adjoining pens standing at attention.

Mounting Pressures

As time went by the satanic angels kept increasing Sharon and Deborah's workload and placed greater demands upon their time. At times they would arrive home exhausted from a whole day of shoplifting, and as soon as they finished their evening meal, Leo would get a message from an angel saying that they were to go out again that day and do some tire slashing. The angel said that God wanted to bring hardship on "totaled" individuals.

At this time I should say that Leo had allegedly been given the ability to sort out cars that belonged to such "totaled" individuals. He said that right above the automobile would hang a small black cloud.

To understand the kind of pressures the Halstead sisters were under, let's look at more of Deborah's interrogation under oath:

"Q: Do you know how many times approximately that you went out on tire slashing or popping?

"A: A lot of times. Sometimes it would be like he would have us going in the stores all day long and we'd be exhausted when we got home at night and think we can relax now, and he'd say, 'No, we have to go out and do tires.' And sometimes that would happen, you know, two or three nights in a row.

"Q: Did you ever, you know, say to Leo: 'Hey, now, this isn't right; we shouldn't be doing this'?

"A: Sure, we'd say it all the time to him.

"Q: And what would be his response?

"A: That we had to do it; if we didn't we'd go totaled.

"Q: How did that make you feel when he would tell you that you're going to be totaled?

"A: Frightened. At other times he would say we had to do it in order to keep the Strange Woman and Satan bound in the pit, or they would be freed and come back and kill us.

"Q: OK.

"A: Here we were exhausted from a whole day of shoplifting and he'd say we had to do it, and we'd say, 'Well, how many do we have to do?' and he'd say, 'Well, we have to do 30.'

"Q: What type of places would you go to?

"A: Sometimes he would direct us before we left the house a specific place to go, and other times he'd say, 'Just drive and I'll tell you.'

"Q: Car lots sometimes?

"A: In a car lot it would be because whoever had the car lot was totaled.

"Q: You actually popped some in broad daylight?

"A: Yeah.

"Q: Well, what I'm getting at, Deborah, is if . . .

"A: Nobody ever saw us that we know of. Nobody to our knowledge ever tried to point us out or anything like that. Yeah, we'd do it in broad daylight, shopping centers.

"Q: What kind of noise would that make?

"A: A hissing sound, the air" *(ibid.)*.

THE FATAL NIGHT

Demonic spirits appearing and claiming to be Christ's angels pressed the little group into constant physical action as a means of reducing their ability to reason and function effectively. The beings intended to fill the men's and women's minds with a fear of being lost, a powerful human motivating force. In addition, the fallen angels determined to break down their sense of right and wrong, preparing them to do horrifying things when commanded to do so, such as killing people.

Mr. Paul Frasier, deputy district attorney of Josephine County, on September 26, 1989, at the sentencing hearing of Sharon Lee Halstead, submitted to the court a statement that presented in a precise manner the extent of the crimes committed by the defendant. Here are some excerpts from it:

"On November 5, 1988, at Leo's direction, the Halstead group took another motorcycle from Grants Pass Suzuki, and placed it in the storage locker on Rogue River Highway. On that same day, Leo directed that the Greene family must be destroyed. A plan was discussed wherein the family would be removed from their home and taken somewhere else to be destroyed. The group then went to the D Street Payless in Grants Pass and stole some toy handcuffs. These were to be used in restraining the Greene family while being transported to the site where they were to be destroyed.

"Between 9:00 and 9:30 p.m. the Halstead group went to the Greene family home. After watching some television, Harry and Sharon went to the bathroom. Harry wrote on the wall, 'Trust in Jesus.' Deborah and Leo went into the bathroom later. Leo [also] scribbled on the wall.

"Dave, Lynn, and Nathaniel Greene were at the dining room table. Mr. and Mrs. Greene were paying bills. Nathaniel was seated in a booster chair playing with some toys. Mrs. Greene went into the kitchen and from there could see the writing on the wall in the bathroom. She became upset and asked who was writing on the wall. When no one confessed, she ordered the group to leave. At this point, at Leo's apparent direction, Sharon pulled the gun stolen by Leo from Tex Shively.

"The Greene family at this time was grouped around the dining room table. Lynn Greene said, 'I hope this is a joke.' Harry responded, 'It's not a joke, it's real, and it's loaded.' Deborah took a portable telephone off the dining room table and placed it out of reach of the Greene family. According to David Greene, Sharon made gestures with the gun that Dave interpreted as meaning Sharon wanted to group the family in the living room area adjacent to the dining room.

"David Greene exited the residence at this time by the sliding glass door located by the dining room table. Sharon Halstead followed David out the door and shot him once in the back as he attempted to go and summon help. David Greene was able to get up off the ground after being shot, and stumbled to a neighbor's residence.

"Sharon reentered the residence. Lynn Greene was semi-restrained by Deborah Halstead. . . . Sharon shot Lynn once in the chest. . . . Lynn fell to her knees, and Sharon Halstead shot her again in the top of the head. . . . Lynn was killed instantly by the head wound. Sharon then went to the table where Nathaniel [the Greenes' son] was still seated. . . . She shot Nathaniel in the face once. Nathaniel survived, but is paralyzed from the chest down.

"The Halstead group exited the house and went to the truck. Sharon drove away. While driving, they saw the wounded David Greene collapsed at his next-door neighbor's. Leo stated that the bullet had 'gone through and wiped out his kidneys,' and that 'he had fallen and died.' Deborah picked up the weapon used in the killings of both Marston Lemke and Lynn Greene . . . and reloaded the weapon with ammunition that was in the truck.

"The group then drove to the city of Rogue River. Sharon called the I Street house and asked her parents to unlock the back door; then they returned to Grants Pass. . . .

"David Greene, Jr., who survived, gave the police the description of what occurred, and the Halstead group was arrested at approximately 6:00 a.m. on November 6, 1988, without incident" (statements of facts and scope of crime of the presentence report).

DECEIVED

At her presentence interview Sharon Halstead stated that her attorney had advised her not to discuss the circumstances of the crimes. When asked how she felt now about what had happened, she stated that she wanted the judge to know that she was extremely sorry for her actions and felt frustrated that she could not change anything. She believed that she had been greatly deceived, especially by Lynn Greene and her husband, David, and viewed the Greenes' child as the only innocent person involved. Sharon said she felt terrible and "gets shaky inside" when she realized that the boy must go through his life crippled.

It seems strange to her now that she and others could have believed the teachings of the Greenes, but the couple had told all their followers not to talk to any pastor, as the clergy could not really understand the deep things of God. To do so would only confuse people and create a lot of misunderstanding. Lynn, Sharon said, had told her that demons now controlled Tex Shively and that she must stay away from him.

As brought out in a previous chapter, Mrs. Greene was not the only person to die because of the little group following evil spirits.

"MC MINNVILLE—A missing pickup, possibly pulling a trailer with a horse in it, was being sought by Yamhill County authorities Friday in connection with the death of a 58-year-old man whose bullet-riddled body was found about noon Thursday in a travel trailer near Newberg.

"Dead of multiple gunshot wounds is Marston 'Mike' Lemke, who lived in the trailer at 17596 NE. Olds Lane, Newberg. The property, which also contains a horse arena and barn, is about four miles west of Newberg. A 1988 red Chevrolet pickup with Oregon license NZL274, a two-horse trailer, and a horse were missing from the property 'coincidentally' with the shooting of Lemke, according to John Collins, Yamhill County district attorney. . . .

"An autopsy by the state medical examiner's office Friday confirmed that Lemke's death was caused by 'multiple gunshot wounds.' . . . The Yamhill County sheriff's office Friday was trying to locate relatives of Lemke, who lived alone.

"Collins said he thought that a .38-caliber handgun had

killed Lemke, although the police advisory that listed the missing vehicle as stolen stated that it contained a rifle, shotgun, and ammunition for both" (Portland *Oregonian,* Nov. 5, 1988).

Law enforcement agencies soon linked the Greene and Lemke killings.

"Two sisters accused in the shooting of a Grants Pass family Saturday night were scheduled for arraignment today on murder and attempted murder charges. Yamhill County authorities are also looking at Sharon Halstead, 36, and Deborah Halstead, 31, both of 414 SE. I Street, in connection with the slaying of a man near Newberg Thursday.

"The victims in the local shooting were Lynn Greene, 32, a special education teacher who was pronounced dead at the scene; her husband, David Greene, Jr., 31, a dental technician who was in fair condition today at South Oregon Medical Center; and their [3]-year-old son, Nathaniel, who was in critical condition today at Rogue Valley Medical Center in Medford. They all lived at 902 SE. Fern Street, where the shooting took place about 9:40 p.m. Saturday.

"The motive for the shootings wasn't known this morning. The Halstead sisters were to be arraigned in Josephine County District Court at 1:00 p.m. today. Sharon Halstead has been charged with four counts of aggravated murder, one count of murder, two counts of attempted murder, and two counts of first-degree assault, according to the district attorney's office. Deborah has been charged with one count of murder, two counts of attempted murder, and two counts of first-degree assault.

"Police began looking for Sharon Halstead and a red truck immediately after talking to the wounded David Greene Saturday night. Officers located a red Chevrolet truck a short time later near the Halstead house on I Street. A computer check revealed that the truck, a horse trailer, and a horse had disappeared from a ranch near Newberg at the same time a horse wrangler was found dead of gunshot wounds Thursday. . . .

"Grants Pass police staked out the truck and the Halstead home and then called for the assistance of the Josephine County sheriff's SWAT team. Officers evacuated the neighborhood, and the SWAT team took into custody the six residents of the home about 5:30 a.m. Sunday. Police said Sharon Halstead was booked into jail on a homicide charge. Her sister was charged several hours later. Two other adults were released, and Sharon Halstead's two sons, ages 12 and 9, were placed in the custody of the state children's services division. They were supposedly with their mother when the shootings took place, according to the district attorney's office.

"Bob Stalcup, who lives across the street from the Greenes, said he was working in his computer room when he heard three shots fired in rapid succession. Stalcup then heard someone at his front door yelling for help. This turned out to be David Greene. By the time Stalcup scrambled into his clothes and opened the door, David had already fled to another neighbor's home, leaving behind a pool of blood on his porch.

"As Stalcup was calling 911, Evelyn Drake, who lives immediately to the south of the Greenes, was looking through her peephole in the door. She said she recognized David and opened the door. As soon as she opened the door he collapsed on her living room floor.

"According to Stalcup, Officer Mike Sweeley arrived at the scene within three minutes and asked Greene if he knew who shot him. Stalcup said that he didn't hear the name uttered by David, but that Greene also said something to the effect of 'They were friends; why would they do this?' . . .

"Stalcup said he went inside the Greenes' house with the officers. Lynn Greene's body was next to the picture window. It appeared she had been kneeling when she was shot, he said. Nathaniel Greene was sitting in his high chair, which was pulled up to the table. The youngster had been shot through the chin and neck. . . . Nathaniel underwent surgery to remove bullet fragments, police said. He may be paralyzed, though, according to a family friend. . . .

"Saturday night, police set up surveillance around the Halsteads' house while plans were being made at the police station and search warrants were being drawn up at the district attorney's office. Police set up a command post . . . and the SWAT team started moving into position about 1:30 a.m. About 4:30 a.m. police started contacting neighbors, asking them to evacuate to the nearby boys' and girls' club. Several people refused to go, and others didn't respond to the officer's knocking on the door.

"The sheriff's hostage negotiations team phoned the Halstead home about 5:30 a.m., and SWAT members took each occupant of the house out separately. They walked them two houses to the west and made them lie facedown in the grass until the house was secured. . . . Detectives seized a rifle from inside the Halstead house and impounded the red Chevrolet truck reportedly stolen near Newberg" (Grants Pass *Daily Courier,* Nov. 7, 1988).

" 'The experience of being awakened at 5:30 in the morning wasn't that bad,' said one of the . . . parents, 'but being forced by the SWAT people to lie facedown on the wet grass with your hands tied behind your back, and your nose sensing the odor of cat feces that appeared to have been deposited not long before, served to impress me with the reality that our lives were not ours anymore. That experience came upon us as an overwhelming surprise, and changed our lives forever' " *(ibid.).*

As I conversed with this particular parent during April 1996 I realized as never before that living free in a world in which Satan and his angels constantly seek to bring trouble and suffering upon us should always lead us to rejoice in God's protection and goodness, and praise Him for having kept us so many times from the hand of the destroyer.

CHAPTER TEN

LIBERTIES LOST

I t came upon them with the force of a tornado, and was totally unexpected. Those bright angels they had conversed
with for a number of years, the Halstead sisters now began
to realize, were in actuality lying spirits. Satan had suddenly decided to destroy some of the people whom he had
intended to use to divide the Seventh-day Adventist
Church, but who, instead of working to convince and convert
other Adventists to their "new light," had decided to keep it to
themselves and let no one hear about it.

We have no way of really knowing why the fallen angels
abandoned the Greenes, but it is my personal belief that Lynn
Greene had not worked as hard as and in the manner they had
wanted her to, and for that reason decided to have her killed.

To some readers such a statement may sound harsh and even
cruel, but let me tell you something that I discovered during the
time that I was affiliated with the elite society of spirit worshipers.

A number of times I had been highly impressed with some of
the exploits the other spirit worshipers had accomplished with the
aid of Satan's angels; then later on I was shocked to learn that many
of the same individuals had met with violent deaths. And what was
most disturbing was that many times the high priest would blame
those individuals for having brought the great master's displeasure
upon themselves by "some stupid mistake, or by being too timid,
or cowardly" in the presence of trouble. "They brought destruction
upon themselves, and deserved it," he would say.

In one particular case a spirit worshiper was decapitated in a
terrible car accident. To my horror the priest claimed that the

great master (Satan) had planned it that way for some good reason. I got the impression that the priest felt obligated to say something that would make people think well of their supernatural master. He would always protest that Satan dealt fairly with people in his service, arguing that when the great conflict was over and the inhabitants of the galaxies recognized Satan as the only god and legal ruler of this planet, then he would resurrect those individuals and honor them for the part they had in advancing his kingdom. Each of them would receive appropriate rewards.

The newspapers continued to report on the Greenes' condition.

"A youngster left paralyzed by the shooting that also killed his mother Saturday night in Grants Pass was scheduled for surgery today [November 10, 1988] because of complications. Meanwhile, a representative of his family's church expressed sorrow and sympathy for the David Greene family, but also said the church won't turn its back on the alleged assailants, who were also members.

"Nathaniel Greene, who is nearly 3 years old, showed some improvement, and his condition was upgraded to serious two days after he was hospitalized at Rogue Valley Medical Center with a gunshot wound to the chin and neck. However, his condition was downgraded to critical Wednesday morning, a hospital spokeswoman said.

"His father, David Greene, Jr., who was shot in the back during the attack, said Wednesday that his son was having difficulty breathing and was increasingly weary from his struggle to get enough oxygen. He indicated the purpose of the surgery would be to help the tot breathe better.

"Lynn Greene, Nathaniel's mother and David's wife, was killed in the shooting, which took place at their home at 902 SE. Fern Street. The shooting was preceded by conversations about whether one of the suspect's sons had been receiving messages from God.

"Funeral services for Lynn Greene, a 32-year-old special education teacher, were held Wednesday night at the Seventh-day Adventist church in Grants Pass.

"The alleged assailants are Sharon Halstead, 36, and Deborah Halstead, 31, both of 414 SE. I Street. The sisters, childhood friends of David Greene, are being held in jail on murder charges.

"Jay E. Prall, director of communications for the Oregon Conference of the Seventh-day Adventist Church, told reporters Wednesday night the parents of David Greene and the Halstead sisters had been friends for years and longtime members of the church. David Greene, Lynn Greene, Sharon Halstead, and Deborah Halstead were all members of the Grants Pass Seventh-day Adventist congregation, although the Greenes were very active, while the Halsteads attended church infrequently.

"'As members of the Seventh-day Adventist community, our collective hearts reach out in sympathy to David and Nathaniel Greene. We praise God that their lives were spared.' According to Prall, it will be the church's responsibility to help the Greenes put their lives back together after the tragedy. But at the same time, the church can't turn its back on the Halstead sisters, who were still members of the church family, Prall said.

"'Though there can be no tolerance for behavior that leads to crimes such as the Halsteads have been charged with, there must be a spirit of love and an acceptance of individuals,' Prall said.

"Disciplinary action against the Halstead sisters by the church is a possibility, but probably wouldn't be considered unless they are convicted, Prall said" (Grants Pass *Daily Courier,* Nov. 10, 1988).

A month later the Halsteads were again in the *Daily Courier.*

"A hearing Thursday for two sisters accused of shooting a Grants Pass family ended with bail on one being at $550,000, while the other continued to be held without bail. After hearing evidence about the crime, Judge Gerald Neufeld set bail for Deborah Halstead, but ruled against her sister, Sharon Halstead. However, there was no indication in court that Deborah Halstead would be able to come up with the amount required for her release.

"The sisters . . . have been charged with aggravated murder in the shooting of the David Greene, Jr., family November 5. Lynn Greene, 32, was pronounced dead at the scene. Her son, Nathaniel, who is nearly 3, was left paralyzed from the chest down, and David Greene, Jr., 31, is recovering from a gunshot wound to the back. . . .

"The Josephine County district attorney's office asked that both sisters be held without bail. But to do so, the state had to prove there was 'clear and convincing' evidence of guilt. . . . Once the judge ruled he would allow bail for Deborah Halstead, Deputy District Attorney Paul Frasier argued for a high amount. He also handed the judge a copy of a seven-count indictment from Yamhill County that accuses the two sisters of the murder of a Newberg ranch hand November 3, and six other crimes.

"Judge Neufeld used the same evidence brought out during the hearing for Deborah Halstead to rule against Sharon Halstead in her release hearing. After ordering she be held without bail, Neufeld set her next court appearance for Monday, when she is expected to enter a plea" *(ibid.,* Dec. 7. 1988).

THE HIGH COST OF LOST LIBERTIES

The loss of liberty comes in many ways. In this case, for instance, the Halstead sisters found themselves under the restraints of the laws of the land. David Greene, Jr., because of his injuries, lost the capacity to live a normal life, and his son Nathaniel, now 11 years old, is still paralyzed from the chest down.

Dr. Jeffrey Louie's description of the injuries Nathaniel Greene suffered illustrates some of the price the child paid.

"Q: . . . Doctor, . . . would you please describe to the court the injuries that you observed that Nathaniel Greene had suffered?

"A: Well, the external injuries I think are quite obvious. . . . More importantly, a puncture wound in the neck where the bullet had entered his neck. This type was—a tube was sent down his throat into his lungs so we could breathe for him. We got a tube in his bladder so we could make sure urine was coming out. Though these injuries are quite graphic, more important were the injuries you could not see.

"Q: Would you describe the injuries you could not see for us?

"A: This was . . . unfortunate. The child could not move his legs at all, in any manner . . . he was totally paralyzed in his legs. . . . [In addition,] he did not have normal rectal tone. That was part of the injury. He has no control over his bowel function. And it appeared that he had a complete injury to his spinal cord at that time, and what that means [is that] the chance of his ever walking was essentially none.

"Q: Did you subsequently operate on Nathaniel Greene?

"A: Yes, I did.

"Q: . . . Could you describe the surgery . . . the damage that you saw as you were removing this bullet?

"A: Nathaniel had two surgeries. I was not involved in the first surgery. That was in the portion of his neck to see if he had any injury to the artery to his brain, but he subsequently developed a continuous leak of brain fluid out of his neck into his lung, which was quite a problem. . . . At that time we elected to remove the bullet. . . . Then we made an incision over the second and third portion in his back . . . to expose the covering of the spinal cord which had a tear in it, and obviously the bullet had hit with such impact it had torn the covering of the spinal cord and brain fluid was leaking out. . . . The bullet had gone through the body of the spine and had cut through the nerves to the chest, and I took a clip and clipped it so that it would not leak . . . and I repacked some muscle to keep it from leaking, hopefully, and we cleaned the injury and closed.

"Q: You have seen Nathaniel Greene in the courthouse?

"A: Yes.

"Q: Based on the damage you saw at the time you operated and so forth, do you have a prognosis on whether he will ever be able to walk again or regain the bodily functions you have described that he has lost?

"A: I also discussed this with Dr. Beyers, who is taking care of his rehabilitation, and from her descriptions and what I see today, I don't think he will ever walk again, or move or feel, or have control of his bowel and bladder, or any useful sexual function" (Circuit Court of the State of Oregon court transcripts, vol. 101).

Beware of Angels

The Aching Heart of a Grieving Parent

From the time that Satan brought sin into our world, he has tried to destroy all that brings peace, contentment, and comfort. His eternal object is to fill human hearts with sadness. David Greene, Jr., came to know firsthand that grief. He described to the court one of the darkest days of his life.

"Q: Mr. Greene, under the statute you have the ability or the right to address the court and tell the court how you feel and how this incident has had an impact on you and what you think ought to be done, so if you would like to at this time, you can address the court and tell the court how you feel about this.

"A: OK. I'll try to read this without taking too long. Not knowing how to describe or how someone else feels in terms of pain, the thoughts and situations that flow through my mind, that exist today and will continue on for days and years to come. Nathaniel has scars on his face. These are Nathaniel's visible scars. I see those visible scars and picture him sitting there watching her pull the trigger. I think of the invisible scars. There are scars you cannot see now. Many say the pain will go away, but only those that have not had this kind of pain. It will always hurt to watch Nathaniel cry in frustration. Five times a day he must be cathed and manually stimulating [*sic*] his bowels every morning. I always miss him climbing in bed or in my lap to snuggle with Mommy and Daddy. Many make excuses for things they do, but no one can take the power of choice. Many during war are tortured and do things they don't want to do and never give in. It would not have been done if they did not want to do it. Can you do anything you want because you believe it? . . . Every day is a reminder to me that something happened that really has no reason. I have the screams of death of one you love—to have the screams of death of one you love echo in your mind the rest of your life. Even time will never dull the memory. To watch the limp little legs wither around like a snake's body without a head. How many here today have had to answer the question I want my mommy, where is my mommy?

"Q: Mr. Greene, would you just prefer to have that statement given to the court?

"A: No. Then nobody will hear it. If you have the patience, I'll get through it.

"Q: OK.

"A: The first powder burns on his face, struggling to breathe. I couldn't even speak the words. Only Nathaniel knows what it's like to lie in a bed for 45 days with a tube in his mouth and not being able to say one word. Does a little boy have to see his mommy die? A person that does crimes to children has no human feelings. The human race would be extinguished. Every day seems to be a dream. People say things; I don't know what to say. Six, seven, or less hours of sleep. Days that can't start until noon. Lifting, lifting everywhere we go. The wheelchair is sure to follow. A tricycle that sits idle, rusting in the backyard. A sandbox with weeds. Favorite plastic toys fading in the sun, covered with spiderwebs. . . . Pictures of times past, of a loving mommy who does not exist. Christmas will go by with no bicycles, scooters, or soccer balls to be seen. Where is Daddy's little helper in the yard to help me? No more curious little eyes peering close to see what project Daddy may be doing around the house. No more chasing Nathaniel until he can't run around the yard anymore because he's laughing so hard. I don't see that kind of laugh very often anymore. Have you ever missed little ones running up to you to hug you? When we go to the park, what are we to play on? How do you play? No more little songs by the sweet, soft voice while taking a bath. Little muddy shoes and socks and pants sitting by the back door. Little fingerprints all over the doorjambs. Boxes of little clothes sorted out for the next baby that used to be worn by Nathaniel. Where a day to go out and play for exercise is to go roll around the stores or the mall. Have you ever watched a 3-year-old grab a hospital bed railing and shake them in frustration, or beating on legs that are there but aren't because they don't work? . . . Or you know what it means to never have the freedom to live normally again? . . . To be alone, to rip the carpet up and see lots of blood of someone you have loved and held hands with, laughed with, that I always wanted to be around? Have you ever cried for three months straight, sometimes so hard your nose bleeds? And now I have to sit up here and say these things and maybe answer questions that won't change anything. You may be able to blacken my reputation, but you can't blacken my character. To me this was a crime of greed. Many things were stolen, including a wife, a mother, a daughter, happiness and futures in the lives of four families. This is not evidence you can see, but they were stolen. Death should be met with death is my feeling, but death is the easy way out, and in this case life of just existing would be best. The court may not see enough evidence for conspiracy, but in my mind and many others', if you find anything at all, then it exists.

"Q: Do you have anything else, Mr. Greene, you would like to tell the court?

"A: Maybe later. Not at this time" *(ibid.)*.

"The mountains shall depart, and the hills be removed; but my kindness shall not depart from thee, neither shall the covenant of my peace be removed, saith the Lord that hath mercy on thee" (Isa. 54:10).

CHAPTER ELEVEN

FACING
HARSH REALITY

M ore than five years had passed since angels had first appeared to the members of the "new light" group. During those years Jesus had supposedly visited Lynn Greene a number of times, declaring she and her followers to be His very special people on earth whom He would use to accomplish wonders in behalf of His commandment-keeping people during the closing earth's history.

One particular day Lynn Greene allegedly received a message from God, brought to her by the "Angel of the Future," regarding two of what he said were God's special people, one being Sharon Lee Halstead. The angel had said:

"Disciples of the Lord, I come before you bearing words from the throne. . . . The future holds much for you; great obstacles will you overcome in the name of Jesus. Walls will fall by your hands. The sun will shine at your words, the earth will stop its turning by your command, all in the name of Jesus. You will walk across the sea to distant lands; your tongues will be many. And at the end of your long journey will await your prize. Will you walk through to the end? For by your sense of time it is long awaiting. Will you live your life in preparation and waiting for this time? Will you remain standing? This is the will of the Lord.

"Sharon, your name is that the Lord has given. . . . Your life will be made new here on this earth before the passing of much time. You, Joseph, with your bare hands will hold back the greatest wave from the sea for many to pass under. And you, Sharon, the shout of your voice will cause the greatest mountain to crumble on your enemy to protect the Lord's people."

As I conversed with Sharon and Deborah at the women's penitentiary in Salem, Oregon, I was impressed with the sincerity with which they had embraced what they believed to be God's will for their lives.

"I was deeply moved," Sharon said to me, "at the thought that God had selected me to do a work for Him that would measure up to that done in ages past by the great people we read about in the Scriptures."

I asked her if the messages given her by the angel had seemed to be too good to be true. Her reply was a yes, adding that for a number of nights it was difficult for her to get to sleep as she pictured in her mind the glorious things she would be doing for the Lord as a leader vested with special power. But now she found herself being interviewed by someone who would tell not of great conquests she had done for God, but of having been misled and cheated of all the freedom she had ever known, and of almost losing out on eternity by giving up all belief in God.

Both sisters were neatly dressed and groomed in their prison garb, and both Hilda and I were surprised at their cheerfulness and the way they have adjusted to the severity of prison life. In fact, while we visited I thanked our Lord in my heart many times for the divine grace and strength His Holy Spirit is imparting to the sisters to keep them from falling apart in such an environment. It had not always been the case. At one time they had thought of ending their lives.

"The younger of two sisters charged in the November shooting deaths of a Grants Pass teacher and a Newberg ranch hand was sentenced Monday to concurrent 20-year terms.

"Deborah Halstead, 32, of Grants Pass, must serve at least 40 months in prison before being eligible for parole under terms of the sentence handed down by Yamhill County Circuit Court judge Donald R. Blensly in McMinnville. . . .

"Deborah Halstead wasn't as culpable as her sister in the killings, Yamhill County district attorney John Collins told the judge Monday. The evidence didn't show her with the weapon or actively participating in either crime, he said.

"Josephine County deputy district attorney Paul Frasier agreed with Collins that Deborah Halstead was less involved. Frasier also told the judge she had agreed to give a statement on the killings. Frasier said Lynn Greene's mother was devastated by the loss of her only daughter and wanted to make sure justice was done. Frasier said the plea agreement negotiated by the state will allow that to happen because it will make more evidence available.

"Frasier also said David Greene also wanted Deborah Halstead to serve as much time as possible and, for that reason, didn't want restitution. Nor does Deborah Halstead have the financial means to make restitution anyway, Collins added. According to parole board rules, a large amount of restitution is considered a mitigating factor that can lead to an early release. . . .

"Also on Monday Frasier read an entry from Lynn Greene's journal in which she wrote about going to the park with her son in October 1987 and watching him play with the ducks.

"'He ran as fast as he could toward me, his hair blowing in the wind with the biggest smile on his face and 100 ducks following behind him.' That image would remain a wonderful memory for the rest of her life, she wrote . . .

"Blensly said he was confronted with the tragedy Deborah Halstead had helped inflict on two innocent people. Saying that the aftermath of the crime would affect the survivors forever, the judge imposed the maximum sentence possible, which is 20 years in prison. Deborah Halstead was given the opportunity to speak on Monday, but declined, Frasier said.

"In an interview Monday, Collins explained the reasoning for setting what seems to be a low minimum sentence for Deborah Halstead. The 40 months is the maximum amount of time she is likely to serve, based on her matrix score. Staying within the matrix makes it more likely the state parole board will leave the sentence alone. The board has the ability to shorten or lengthen prison terms, he added.

"The matrix score, which is determined by the severity of the crime and the individual's criminal record, is used to determine how long an individual will actually stay in Oregon's over-crowded prisons" (Grants Pass *Daily Courier,* June 13, 1989).

"Deborah Halstead chose to say nothing Monday afternoon before she was sentenced to two concurrent 20-year prison terms for conspiring to commit murder in two counties" (McMinnville *News Register,* June 14, 1989).

"Sharon Halstead's aggravated murder case will be moved out of southern Oregon because extensive pretrial publicity would prevent her from getting a fair trial here, a judge ruled today. Josephine County Circuit Court judge Gerald Neufeld said he would try to keep the same trial date of September 12, but could not say where the trial would be held.

"Neufeld made the ruling after hearing the results of a public opinion survey that showed 81 percent of Josephine County and Jackson County residents were familiar with the case and a majority of them thought she was guilty.

"Halstead's attorneys, Kenneth Hadley, of Toledo, and Griffith Steinke, of Newberg, also presented testimony showing considerable community involvement in the case because of a fund-raiser for one of her alleged victims.

"The 36-year-old Halstead is accused of killing Grants Pass teacher Lynn Greene, 32, and wounding her husband, David Greene, and their young son, Nathaniel. David Greene, 31, re-covered, but the 3-year-old Nathaniel is paralyzed from the chest down. . . . Halstead is accused of murdering Newberg ranch hand Mike Lemke on November 2. Prosecutors in both Josephine and Yamhill counties are seeking the death penalty.

"Sharon Halstead's younger sister, Deborah Halstead, 32, also was originally charged with aggravated murder in connection with the killings. However, she pleaded no contest in May to two charges of conspiracy to commit murder and was sentenced in June to 20 years in prison.

"Speaking to the court by phone from New York this morning, Eugene pollster Thomas English said his interviewers questioned 305 people in Josephine County and 300 people in Jackson County. Thomas said that 63 percent of the Josephine County respondents had already decided Sharon Halstead was guilty. Of those, 43 percent believe she should receive the death penalty following a fair trial, he said. 'It's apparent that half of the eligible jury members (in both counties) have a prejudiced view because of extensive media coverage,' English said.

"The defense also presented considerable testimony about a fund-raiser conducted by employees of the Royale Gardens health-care facility to benefit Nathaniel Greene. Defense investigators videotaped two events in which the youngster participated, as well as numerous posters advertising the fund-raiser that eventually brought in $18,000.

"In explaining his decision after the hearing, the judge said it was his job to make sure that Sharon Halstead received a fair trial. The publicity alone, as judged by survey, would be enough to move the case, Neufeld said. But an additional factor he had to consider was the amount of community involvement in the effort to help Nathaniel. Neufeld said the fund-raisers weren't at fault for moving the case and didn't want to discourage people from making similar efforts in the future" (Grants Pass *Daily Courier,* July 6, 1989).

CHAPTER TWELVE

THE COURT SEEKS HELP

In their effort to understand the events that had led to the Greene/Lemke tragedies, the Circuit Court of the State of Oregon felt that the best help they could get would come to them from the Adventist Church, and it appealed to the president of the Oregon Conference of Seventh-day Adventists for its assistance. Elder Larry Evans was asked to testify in court under oath.

"Mr. Hadley: Mr. Evans, for the record, would you state your name, please?

"A: Larry Robert Evans.

"Q: How do you spell your last name?

"A: E-v-a-n-s.

"Q: What is your profession or occupation?

"A: I'm currently the special assistant to the president of the Oregon Conference of Seventh-day Adventists.

"Q: Can you tell us what that job entails in general terms?

"A: OK. Probably three broad categories. One, I'm a church consultant, so I work with churches in assisting them spiritually and to grow numerically as well. I also am director of the multicultural ministries. I work with various ethnic groups, but specifically here I am responsible to the president and assigned projects, and one of those projects is working with independent ministries, sometimes called offshoots.

"Q: Is that kind of what we're talking about this afternoon?

"A: I would say this definitely falls into that category.

"Q: Backing up somewhat, what is your history with the church?

"A: I've been a pastor for about 15 years. In various kinds of departmental work, working with independent churches for three years, and in administration now for about two.

"Q: Where is your office?

"A: In Clackamas—Portland.

"Q: You are here under subpoena; is that correct?

"A: That's correct.

"Q: Under that subpoena I left with you certain records concerning David Greene, Sr., and David Greene, Jr.; is that correct?

"A: Yes.

"Q: I think you called me this morning; you were two hours out of Portland without some records?

"A: Yes. I had studied those the night before.

"Q: I indicated you shouldn't go back to Portland?

"A: Correct.

"Q: When did you first become aware of this group in the Grants Pass area that we have been talking about here this afternoon?

"A: This specific group I was not really made aware of by names until probably after the shooting.

"Q: Speaking of David Greene, Sr., had you become familiar with his writings?

"A: I had heard the name, I suppose, and there were a number of independent groups in the southern Oregon Adventists and otherwise, and I had in fact come down and visited with a group of some of these independents in the Canyonville area. These individuals I do not recognize, but that was about two, two and a half years ago.

"Q: Are you familiar with the terms the voice ministry and deliverance ministry?

"A: Yes, I'm well acquainted with the idea of thought voice and deliverance ministries.

"Q: Would you describe what those terms mean to you?

"A: I think we have heard it today. Deliverance ministry is an emphasis on the casting out of demons out of individuals who have, quote, been possessed of devils. Thought voice basically is a

137

communication between an individual and a superior being. In this case it would be usually an angel.

"Q: Correct me if I'm wrong; I believe you indicated to an investigator that this concept of talking with the angels is kind of a questionable concept within the church; is that right?

"A: Yes.

"Q: If I'm putting you on the spot or asking you something you can't really speak for the church, please say so.

"A: Well, it's clear that this is certainly an aberration. The Seventh-day Adventist Church does not endorse this. We have groups who are doing this, but not in harmony with the Seventh-day Adventist organization.

"Q: That's both the thought voice ministry and the deliverance ministry?

"A: I think the thought voice for sure. Deliverance ministry, there is a section in which the church recognizes that indeed there is an evil power that overcomes and takes great persuasion over individuals. We are very hesitant to go to the lengths by far that has been described today. I think Seventh-day Adventists certainly believe simply that there is a demonic power, there is a heavenly Father, and certainly believe there is a confrontation going on, and we are individuals who have to struggle with those types of temptations. We do believe, though, that it is not necessary to go through a lot of gyrations to ask the devil, these powers, to leave. The phenomena of deliverance ministries developed quite a formula for exorcising these people as seen by other groups, such as the film *The Exorcist.* . . .

"Q: At some point did you receive some of these writings David Greene, Sr., had supposedly prepared?

"A: Yes.

"Q: Can you tell us how they came into your possession?

"A: I guess I'm a collective agency. These things unfortunately seem to come to my office for investigation and for counsel for churches that inquire.

"Q: You indicated you don't have all the papers with you, but what kind of documents did you receive in that regard?

"A: In that regard I have a manuscript that David Greene, Sr., has written, explaining his belief on numerous points—thought voice, exorcism, deliverance ministries. It reveals a lot about what we call hermeneutics or his interpretation principle for deciphering Scripture. In that file we have requested the president, our conference requested, he is the only one who can make that official request in the local conference with our General Conference headquarters in Washington, D.C. What we have there is called the Biblical Research Institute, indicated as BRI. The BRI has a number of theologians who are employed to help decipher and guide the church in some of these theological issues as they arise. The president requested that the Biblical Research Institute review and analyze and give counsel regarding the document, the manuscript that David Greene, Sr., has.

"Q: Did they respond to you or to the president?

"A: Yes.

"Mr. Frasier: Your Honor, I'm going to have to object at this point. I realize the rules of evidence don't apply to these things, but I fail to see the relevancy of this line of questioning to the issues at hand and the sentencing of this defendant. I think I'm going to have to object at this point.

"Mr. Hadley: Your honor, a key issue, of course, is the thinking of the defendant that got her into this predicament, and there has been testimony already that some of these writings were in her possession. . . .

"Mr. Frasier: I think what some church agency in Washington, D.C., did with this material that has not been communicated to the defendant has no relevance to these proceedings.

"The Court: I'll overrule the objection.

"Q: Briefly, Mr. Evans, could you summarize the response from Washington, D.C.?

"A: I'll read an excerpt, if that would be permissible. . . . 'The congregation would be most unwise to place this brother into public office. If he is cultivating a group in deliverance ministries, and latter-rain sanctification perfection, including thought messages and supernatural events, he really should be dismissed from fellowship. Brother Greene's materials are anti-church, as far as the organization is concerned. The doctrine he is teaching is a delusion. His influence on new members would be negative and deceptive if these materials are read and accepted. He apparently does not push his ideas, an attitude which says if you can't accept them, you can die and go to heaven that way, but if you can accept these things, you will be one of the special few that will enjoy these unusual experiences and can be translated without seeing death. Such a pitch will be appealing and deceive some and lead them away from the truth. Error is never harmless. Unless he is willing to give up these strange and confusing views, I don't see how he could be a supportive member. It is evident that he has spent hours and hours in study and has great skills in reasoning and communication, but in some way he has gotten off the track and will draw others with him.'

"Q: What is the date of that, Mr. Evans?

"A: June 6, 1989.

"Q: Obviously that is the first official interpretation of those writings that you are aware of?

"A: Yes.

"Q: You mentioned another group called the Davidians. Are you familiar with a group such as that?

"A: Some.

"Q: What can you tell the court about that? I take it it doesn't tie into this area?

"A: I would really not see it as a direct tie with this case, other than it is a group that doesn't represent the Seventh-day Adventist teaching, nor do their practices, and they also are very independent, will not take counsel from the mother church. I think it would be well for us to say here that we do have some guidelines that have been developed by the church to help these people, these groups, to have representation. I think within the church we want to give latitude, we don't want to put people in a box and say that's what you have to believe, you have to give latitude, but there are some parameters that are drawn, and a guideline has been drawn, and this particular group are flagrant in at least three or four points out of those we have.

"Q: I believe there was mention in some testimony or the record someplace about a J. Reynolds Hoffman being involved with this group for a short time. Are you familiar with that name?

"A: Yes.

"Q: Is he a member of the church?

"A: I think he is a member. In fact, I interviewed him not too long ago. He is making a change. The deliverance ministries in about 1985 began to shift more to thought voice. As they began to move and develop, several of those people began to question what was happening as the thought voice manifestations began to become more formal, more absurd. This phenomenon began to grow among a smaller group, and people like Hoffman have been raising questions, I suppose, within that group of Adventists who are involved in deliverance ministries that would not see the Adventist Church as the one who is inspiring the change relative to former minister . . . Hoffman.

"Q: Is there anything else you would like to add to this? You have heard this afternoon what's been going on.

"A: I think one thing that's important here, at least from my perspective and from our practices, is that this phenomenon is larger than a religious group. It is a phenomenon that now has moved into the secular realm and is affecting other people with violent acts, other than this. And I think this is a significant point in seeing the bigger perspective, the New Age movement, mind and life. Shirley MacLaine, most of the cases . . . [of] people who are of this belief . . . have got what this group called demonic influence. Shirley MacLaine would call it the mind life influence. . . . There is a phenomenon that seems to be sweeping this country that [includes] this out-of-body, out-of-mind experience, leading people to do things that most rational people would not do.

"Q: I take it in this type of group there must be leaders and followers?

"A: There is, and there is a real rivalry among these groups. Power, leadership is something that is really sought after. This is why the church is an enemy to these groups, because the church represents authority. They do not want any religious authority.

They are vying for that. We have splinter groups even in the church and outside the Adventist Church that are vying for recognition and authority. They want to have the last word.

"Mr. Hadley: That's all."

"Mr. Frasier: Sir, I take it from your comments today that within the state of Oregon there have been other instances where you have been called upon to deal with other deliverance ministries and thought voice ministries elsewhere in the state; would that be a fair statement?

"Mr. Evans: Not specific, but rather from a counselor or rescue position, yes, I have been asked questions.

"Q: How many, would you estimate, in the state of Oregon, how many of these type ministries do we have?

"A: I would say I would hope one. I see them all as one group. I don't see them as exceptions.

"Q: We have this group we have been talking about in southern Oregon. They are located elsewhere in the state then?

"A: Yes.

"Q: Yet is it not true that within the boundaries of the state of Oregon this is the only group that you are aware of or part of the ministries you are aware of that have experienced acts of violence?

"A: Yes, as far as I know.

"Q: Now I take it from your comments today, sir, that you have not had any direct contact, personal contact, with Dave Greene, Sr.?

"A: That is correct.

"Q: Or with Dave or Lynn Greene; is that correct?

"A: Correct.

"Q: I take it that you have had no personal contact or direct contact with Sharon Halstead?

"A: That is correct.

"Q: So you can't tell us based on your own personal knowledge if any of these writings of David Greene, Sr., had any affect on this defendant, can you?

"A: I cannot say that directly, no.

"Q: What you read to us from the article in Washington, D.C., none of that was ever communicated to Sharon Halstead prior to November 5, 1988?

"A: The specifics of this were not.

"Mr. Frasier: Thank you. I have nothing further.

"Mr. Hadley: Nothing further" (Circuit Court of the State of Oregon court transcripts, vol. 101).

CHAPTER THIRTEEN

FROM BIBLE STUDY TO SPIRITISM

In testifying under oath in the Circuit Court of the State of Oregon for the County of Josephine, at Grants Pass, Oregon, John Gentry remained on the witness stand for a longer time than any other person. He described in great detail the years he spent with the "new light" group. The other members considered him as one who walked with God. Gentry supposedly had gone to heaven and visited there many times while having out-of-body experiences.

John Gentry provided extremely revealing insights into the way the religious group conducted itself, their attitudes, and their daily life. Their behavior revealed just how far from God Satan's angels had led them while they still believed that God was directing them. The following court transcript chillingly records in the words of someone involved how Satan deceived what at first were sincere Bible students.

"Mr. Steinke: Will you state your full name for the record, and spell your last name, please?

"A: John Martin Gentry, G-e-n-t-r-y.

"Q: Did you ever live next door to a gentleman by the name of Ken Cook?

"A: Yes.

"Q: About when was that?

"A: About '82, '83.

"Q: Did you get to know Mr. Cook at all during this time?

"A: Yes.

"Q: What did he do? His work, what did he do?

"A: Mechanic.

"Q: How did you become involved with him?

"A: I needed something repaired. He fixed it.

"Q: At some point did he invite you to study the Bible with him?

"A: Yes.

"Q: About how long had you known him at that time?

"A: Two weeks.

"Q: Was he married at that time?

"A: Yes.

"Q: Do you recall his wife's name?

"A: Yes.

"Q: What was that?

"A: Denise.

"Q: Did you go over there—how often did you go over there to read the Bible with them?

"A: Two or three nights a week.

"Q: At some point did you expand from—this is just the three of you, right?

"A: Yes.

"Q: At some point did you expand from just the three of you?

"A: Well, sometimes his mother-in-law would come up, or his brother-in-law. But it was always at his house.

"Q: At Ken Cook's house?

"A: Yes.

"Q: At some point did Ken and Denise Cook ask you to go over to Dave and Lynn Greene's home with them?

"A: Yes.

"Q: Was that more Bible reading, Bible study over there?

"A: I believe that's what it was. It was also just to meet them.

"Q: What were the Greenes like when you first met them, do you recall?

"A: They seemed like they were very—they were newlyweds. Real happy.

"Q: Was there a difference between Dave and Lynn? Was one more outgoing than the other?

"A: Lynn was more outgoing.

"Q: Did you eventually begin having Bible studies and Bible readings with the Greenes?

"A: Yes.

"Q: About how often were you doing that?

"A: It would start maybe once a week, and then progressed to two times and three times a week.

"Q: Would this have been back in say, '84, in that general time frame?

"A: Yes.

"Q: How long would each of those sessions go?

"A: An hour, an hour and a half.

"Q: When you first started out, was there any talk about casting out demons, or talking to God, or were these just ordinary reading-the-Bible sort of studies?

"A: It was just basic out-of-the-Bible truth. No casting out spirits.

"Q: Was anybody leading the group at that point?

"A: No.

"Q: Was there a time when Sharon Halstead came to the group?

"A: That was about a month after I met Dave and Lynn.

"Q: Who introduced you to Sharon?

"A: I don't know. I think it was Dave.

"Q: Did she come over during your Bible studies?

"A: Yes.

"Q: Do you recall who drove her there?

"A: No.

"Q: Do you remember somebody by the name of Cheryl Ross?

"A: Yes.

"Q: Who is she, if you recall?

"A: I believe that's Sharon's cousin.

"Q: Did Sharon then join your Bible study group? Perhaps join is the wrong word. Did she start coming more regularly?

"A: Yes. I believe she just moved into town.

"Q: This would have been back in about '84?

"A: Yes.

"Q: Did Cheryl Ross come to some of the meetings?

"A: Only a few of them. I believe she lived up north.

"Q: So then it was yourself and Ken Cook and Denise Cook and Dave and Lynn Greene, and Sharon, and on a few occasions Cheryl Ross; is that right? Did anyone else come from time to time?

"A: Over the years people were introduced into it.

"Q: Was there a fellow by the name of Bud?

"A: Yes.

"Q: Did he come fairly early on?

"A: I don't know. I didn't meet him until later on.

"Q: During this early time back in roughly 1984 . . . you know who Leo and Harry are, don't you?

"A: Yes.

"Q: Who are they?

"A: They're Sharon's children.

"Q: During the early meetings back in 1984 did they come to the meetings?

"A: No.

"Q: Do you know where they were?

"A: I believe their grandmother was baby-sitting.

"Q: At some point in the course of the Bible study with the Greenes and Cooks and Sharon Halstead and Cheryl Ross, did you or your group ever become aware of a Bible study that was taking place up in Canyonville?

"A: Yes.

"Q: Who was the person in Canyonville who was running that study?

"A: Jean Ketzner.

"Q: Was her daughter also involved?

"A: Yes.

"Q: At some point did your group go up to Canyonville to meet Jean Ketzner?

"A: Yes.

"Q: Do you know who first brought up going to Jean Ketzner's in Canyonville?

"A: No, but there was talk of Jean having Bible studies up there. I don't know who brought the idea up to go.

"Q: Was—were you told that there were any special groups this Jean Ketzner had?

"A: Yes.

"Q: What were you told?

"A: That she could directly communicate with God and had the ability to take a—the evil spirits out of a person. Cast them out.

"Q: You were told that before you met her?

"A: Yes.

"Q: When you first went there was that an all-day affair, or two hours? How long were you up there?

"A: About five hours.

"Q: Do you recall what day of the week that was?

"A: It was either Friday or the following day, Saturday.

"Q: Do you recall who went with you?

"A: I believe it was Dave and Lynn, myself, in one car.

"Q: Were Ken and Denise Cook also there?

"A: They might have been.

"Q: Was Sharon present?

"A: I don't remember.

"Q: What happened when you arrived at the Ketzner residence in Canyonville?

"A: They showed us around their house. We might have had something to eat, and then we started talking Bible stuff.

"Q: Who did most of the talking when you got to the religion part?

"A: Jean.

"Q: Did she mention people that she knew back East who were casting out demons?

"A: The first time I was there she didn't.

"Q: Did that come later?

"A: Yes.

"Q: About how many times did you go to the Ketzner place?

"A: About five times.

"Q: Did you ever actually see a meeting in which demons were cast out of people?

"A: Yes.

"Q: Could you describe . . . what happened?

"A: Well, this was in the Ketzners' house, upstairs in a room. There were about seven or eight of us, and Jean was going to take out demons that were troubling this man. They were in him and around about him. And we all prayed the Spirit of God would be with us, and then she would call out the demons that were plaguing this man, and he would become real wild, kind of wild like a person would be if he was on a drug like PCP, like he was in a trance, and he kept saying that he wanted the children to leave the room so they wouldn't get hurt. After about an hour he was supposedly clean, and they wanted to take the void that was in his body of the evilness and put the Holy Spirit into it and make him filled with goodness.

"Q: How did they go about doing that?

"A: Well, I wasn't qualified to be able to cast these demons out. I don't know how they do that.

"Q: Did Jean Ketzner do that?

"A: Yes.

"Q: Did she call them by name?

"A: Yes.

"Q: Do you recall—you said seven or eight people were there. Do you recall who was there?

"A: I can't be sure of the people, but I believe it was myself, it was Richard Flowers, it could have been Ken Cook, Bud, and Vicky and Charles Villegas.

"Q: Vicky is Charles Villegas's daughter, right?

"A: Yes.

"Q: Did she ever acquire the ability to speak directly to God?

"A: Vicky?

"Q: Yes.

"A: I believe she spoke to her companion angel. That was it.

"Q: How old was Vicky?

"A: I don't know. She was a college girl.

"Q: Now's she's in college?

"A: I believe so.

"Q: Was this the only time that you saw the casting out of demons at the Ketzners', or were there other occasions as well?

"A: That was the only one that was so dramatic. The other ones didn't seem like they did anything.

"Q: But there were other occasions?

"A: Just a few.

"Q: Were you baptized at the Ketzners'?

"A: Yes.

"Q: Was anyone baptized with you?

"A: Richard was.

"Q: Richard Flowers. Where were you baptized?

"A: In the backyard in a swimming pool.

"Q: Who performed the baptism?

"A: Ken Cook.

"Q: Am I correct that as you are still going to the Ketzners' occasionally you were still having meetings at Dave and Lynn Greene's house as well?

"A: Yes.

"Q: Did those meetings change in any way after you started going up to the Ketzners'?

"A: Well, at the beginning we were quite often real innocent, but over the months and the years they were less frequent and they were more serious about casting away of demons and the controversy between good and bad.

"Q: Did the group get more and more into what's been referred to as message ministry directed to God and talking to angels, that sort of thing?

"A: Yes.

"Q: Did you change how you even sat at the group meetings?

"A: Yes, we would sit in a circle.

"Q: How had you sat before?

"A: Somebody might sit on the couch, on the floor, or in a chair. Anywhere they felt comfortable.

"Q: Did everyone then have to start sitting on the floor at some point?

"A: Yes.

"Q: Whose idea was that?

"A: Well, I don't know, but it was something we didn't verbally say, we just did. We noticed everyone else was sitting in circles and you joined them.

"Q: At some point did members of your group, and I'm referring to the Greenes and the Cooks and the Halsteads and yourself, those people who were attending that Bible study, did members of that group at some point begin to claim that they could see and hear?

"A: Yes.

"Q: Could you explain to us what we're talking about when we say hearing and seeing, in your own words again? What does that mean to you?

"A: Well, everybody wasn't seeing and hearing the same way. Some people could hear within their mind like their subconscious, where others could hear verbally like you're listening to me now.

"Q: Except that they were talking to angels?

"A: They thought they were. To be able to see, you would close your eyes and pray and supposedly God would be giving you a message, maybe transferring it into you, and you would visually see something appear as if you were in a dream.

"Q: We have heard something about you checking out the spirits to make sure you're talking to the right ones. Do you recall doing that?

"A: Yes.

"Q: How was that done?

"A: There were only two tests that you could use. You want to be sure that you were praying and that you were getting your information from God, not something counterfeit, and you would ask if Jesus had come in the flesh and died on the holy cross, and, I believe, if you accepted Jesus Christ as your personal Lord and Saviour.

"Q: Who asked the questions?

"A: The person that was receiving the message.

"Q: If that person could see, that person would also watch the angel to see how it reacted; is that correct?

"A: Yes.

"Q: What would you look for if you could see?

"A: If it was a counterfeit angel and was Satan, he couldn't look you in the eye, and he would stutter around on the answer. And he would give you the impression that he was a good angel.

"Q: Did the group ever set up spiritual barriers before they began conversing with angels?

"A: Yes.

"Q: How was that done?

"A: We prayed for the holy angels to surround the house, and they would have the [sword] of God's wrath, and in a sense these angels would put a barrier between the outside world and inside the house to prevent evil spirits from coming in. When we did that, it wasn't guaranteed, because Satan himself was supposedly so strong that he could move right in.

"Q: Even through the barriers that you were setting up?

"A: Because we didn't have enough good angels.

"Q: Were the angels armed? Did they have weapons or shields?

"A: They would have a shield, and they probably would have a sword.

"Q: Would it be fair to say that the group began spending less time studying the Bible and more time discussing spirits and spiritualism?

"A: That's all it was in the end.

"Q: Can you put that in a time frame, about when that change started to take place within the group?

"A: It was very gradual. In 1987, that would probably be the strongest year for the group. Everybody was real tight, and the loose members, the ones that started with us from the beginning, that were not seeing eye-to-eye about messages, they were asked not to come anymore, and toward the very end, before the violence happened, each member of the group that used to come together had separated, and they were dealing with God in their own home personally, and there would still be times when a member of the group would have a message that they received from God, and they had to go tell another person, whether they wanted to hear it or not, and you would have to tell these people the message, because if you didn't carry out and be the messenger for God, then you were sinning, so you'd carry out the message or the act that you needed to do.

"Q: You say in 1987, that was the strongest year for the group. Who were the members who were so tight during that time?

"A: It would be myself, Sharon, Bud, Jean, Vicky, and Charles. Ken and Denise Cook never attended.

"Q: What about Dave and Lynn Greene?

"A: We were at their house.

"Q: But you left them out of the list; that's why I asked.

"A: Yes.

"Q: Why did Ken and Denise stop coming to the group?

"A: Now, I'm not certain, because they're both my friends, so I never pried into it, but I believe that—

"Mr. Frasier: Your Honor, I think I'm going to object. If the witness does not know, I don't think he should try to guess.

"The Court: If the witness is going to speculate, he shouldn't answer the question.

"Q: All right. Was there ever a dispute between Ken and Denise Cook and Dave and Lynn Greene that you know of?

"A: Yes.

"Q: Do you know what that was about?

"A: I believe it was the way in which they were checking the spirits.

"Q: At one of the meetings were Ken and Denise Cook asked to leave and not come back?

"A: I wasn't there then.

"Q: OK. Did everyone in the group want to have the ability to see and hear God and the angels directly?

"A: Yes.

"Q: Did you personally ever think that God was talking to you while you were in the group?

"A: I believe that—you see, now that I have more light of what was going on I see it differently, but the still small voice in your head, I believed it was God talking to me.

"Q: At the time you believed it, but since then you have changed your mind?

"A: Yes.

"Q: At some point did the boys, Leo and Harry, begin coming to the group?

"A: Yes.

"Q: Do you recall about when that was?

"A: About a year before Lynn was injured. They would be in the other room, and gradually they started to become more welcome into the Bible study.

"Q: At first they were kept out?

"A: Yes.

"Q: As time went along did you become closer to Sharon personally?

"A: Yes.

"Q: You became boyfriend and girlfriend?

"A: Yes.

"Q: Started dating?

"A: Yes.

"Q: At one point you actually lived together for some time, didn't you?

"A: Yes.

"Q: When did the two of you start living together?

"A: I can't recall what year that was.

"Q: Do you recall about how long you were together?

"A: In the same house living?

"Q: Yes.

"A: I would say about three years.

"Q: Did the two of you have marriage plans?

"A: I did.

"Q: At some point did you buy a ring?

"A: Yes.

"Q: Was there ever a message that came to someone in the

group that interfered with your marriage plans?

"A: Yes.

"Q: Could you tell us about that, again in your own words?

"A: Somebody had received a message that stated that Sharon was to be married to another man and it hadn't taken place, so I didn't do anything, suspecting that when the man did show up she'd give up on it, but over the months that preceded she was so-called married in heaven, her spirit, which meant to me that it was time for me to move out so God wouldn't be mad at me even more for living with her—living with a person that was married. [Author's note: Sharon had been told that she was to marry a former Catholic priest who would come from Europe, and that they would have a child.]

"Q: Do you recall who the message came from?

"A: It was either Lynn or Sharon, because they talked so close together on those kinds of things.

"Q: Among the people in your group, who were the primary ones who were able to hear?

"A: In the very beginning it would have been me and Lynn and Denise. And then toward the end the people that could hear were not telling their messages to other people, and the members that couldn't hear or see would ask questions and they would get answers from them.

"Q: Do you know what I mean when I speak about spiritual travel?

"A: Yes.

"Q: What does that mean in your own words?

"A: The separating of your body from your soul. Supposedly having an out-of-body experience, and then after leaving and doing what the Lord would have you do, to be able to enter back into your body, your physical body, and recall everything that you had done.

"Q: Is that something that the group discussed?

"A: Yes.

"Q: Was that something that was believed in by the members of the group?

"A: Yes.

"Q: Did any members of the group claim to have gone on spiritual journeys?

"A: Yes.

"Q: Which members of the group that you recall claimed to have gone on spiritual journeys.

"A: Vicky, myself, Dave and Lynn and Jean.

"Q: Who was the last one?

"A: Jean Ketzner.

"Q: You say you were one of those who went on a spiritual journey. Could you describe the experience?

"A: Yes.

"Q: Would you do that for us, please?

"A: Well, I had no control of where I was going to be going, but supposedly I went up for seven days' travel to the New City, the City of God, and I went into a gate and the angel was carrying me, and we went around the city and saw things, and the tree of life and the throne of God, and after I had seen all that it turned around and we left through the same gate, and we floated back down to earth, and we went through the ceiling of Dave's house and I entered my body.

"Q: You said you went through the same gate. Did somebody go with you on that journey?

"A: No.

"Q: That was just you?

"A: I believe that the angels didn't believe I could take myself, so they grabbed me and carried me.

"Q: Did members of the group ever go on journeys together, spiritual journeys?

"A: I believe they did. I don't recall that, though.

"Q: After somebody had gone on one of these journeys, would they discuss it with the group when they got back?

"A: Yes.

"Q: Was that a regular topic of conversation?

"A: Yes.

"Q: At this point, and I think we're talking about 1987,

maybe early '88, how often was the group meeting?

"A: It was every two weeks. We'd see each other, though, in church.

"Q: Is anyone in the group questioning the validity of these occurrences, these spiritual journeys or talking to angels or things like that?

"A: I had been questioning it only because Ken Cook had showed me the light, and I could see the failure behind the whole system that we were doing, but since I wasn't outspoken enough, because I didn't want to lose any friends, I said nothing.

"Q: So you did not bring it up in the group itself?

"A: Right.

"Q: At some point does Deborah Halstead come on the scene?

"A: Yes.

"Q: You know who Deborah Halstead is, don't you?

"A: Sharon's sister.

"Q: When did she get involved in all this?

"A: Well, she was—I met her supposedly about eight or nine months after I met Sharon, and she was around town for a while. She left for several years and then she came back about a month before Lynn was hurt.

"Q: When Deborah came back, did that affect your living arrangement with Sharon?

"A: Yes.

"Q: How, in your own words again, how was your arrangement affected?

"A: I was out of there.

"Q: You and Deborah didn't get along?

"A: Not at all.

"Q: Did she ever threaten you?

"A: Yes.

"Q: Do you recall specifically what the threats were?

"A: She was tired of hearing demons talk through my mouth, and she actually laid her hand on my shoulder and pushed me back, and all I did was laugh at her and make things worse. So she turned around and walked away. She did return, and she supposedly had prayed while she was gone, and she said she was sorry.

"Q: Did the two of you ever have a run-in in a store?

"A: That was it.

"Q: That was it? What was that about?

"A: Well, when you're shopping for groceries and you have them in your cart, you're not allowed to eat them before you leave the store, and she [had] already proceeded to drink a little carton of milk, and I noticed it. Harry and Leo had little things of candy and they were going to be doing the same thing, and I just told her point-blank 'I'll turn you in, wrong's wrong and right's right.' That's when she got mad at me.

"Q: Did things change around the house the way the household was run when Deborah came up?

"A: Yes.

"Q: Who was in charge after she arrived?

"A: Well, Sharon would have liked to have been, but Deborah is a real strong-willed person. If you don't do it Deborah's way, you don't do it at all, and I wasn't allowed to come into the house or talk to her ever.

"Q: When you say you were not allowed to talk to her, you mean Sharon?

"A: Debbie.

"Q: How did Leo and Harry, the two boys, react to Deborah's presence in the house?

"A: Well, at first they were glad that she had left the city, and then the old feelings came back that she was being too bossy. As far as I could see, she was giving them gifts, letting them watch movies on the VCR, and she won their hearts over with worldly goods. Soon enough the children would obey Debbie before they would their own mother.

"Q: At some point did Leo Shively, Sharon's son, make a claim that he could hear and see God?

"A: Yes.

"Q: Do you recall approximately when that was?

"A: A month prior to Debbie moving up here.

"Q: Did that coincide with any change in Lynn's ability to hear?

"A: Now, I hadn't been associating with the Greenes.

"Q: You hadn't been?

"A: No.

"Q: Did Leo's claim that he could see and hear God affect the family relationship?

"A: Yes.

"Q: Describe in your own words how it affected that.

"A: Well, when I was still there Leo would come up with a kind of absurd thing that God had told him that he must go do . . . But after hearing what he had said you realized it wasn't from God, because it was not in God's character or nature. It was usually something that was bad that a little kid would think of doing.

"Q: What did Sharon Halstead do when Leo came up with these visions from God?

"A: In the beginning I could see that Sharon was questioning it; then she reasoned with herself, and she must have come to the conclusion that God had told Leo to do this, and she couldn't stop him or she would be meddling with something God wanted done.

"Q: Did the children's play activities change, and specifically I want you to refer to playing with weapons and warfare and things like that.

"A: Yes. It used to be just bicycles and with the skateboards. Toward the beginning of November last year there were—well, they believed they were fully combat-ready little GI Joe people. They had all the camouflage clothing and the makeup, and they were always playing with these toys, as if they were figuring out strategies to be able to take people down.

"Q: Did you ever see them abusing their toys?

"A: Deliberately breaking them?

"Q: Yes; some amputating?

"A: Maybe they would break an arm off a toy soldier, and they would say the toy had been shot by the enemy and they had to amputate its arm off, but they didn't have a lot of toys.

"Q: In terms of whether or not you should stay in the home, which side did Leo take?

"A: Well, Leo for the longest time wanted me to be in the home, but the very last few months he wanted me to leave so that Sharon could marry her new husband.

"Q: Did Leo ever threaten you personally?

"A: Once.

"Q: What did he threaten to do?

"A: I had mentioned to Sharon that she should punish the kid when he gets out of line, and Sharon went to the kitchen. Leo was standing there and he was real mad, and he had mentioned that he would say something to the police that all the cuts and scars that he had on his arms and legs, I had caused them. Child abuse. And I didn't know what to say, so I told him that would never hold up. He then told me that it was then perfectly easy for him to go in the bedroom while I was sleeping and cut my throat, and they couldn't do anything to him because he was under age.

"Q: Did you believe that he would do that?

"A: Well, I was shocked, but I put the dresser in front of the door just in case. The kids would stay up a lot longer than adults do, playing around.

"Q: You also took it seriously enough to take some precautions?

"A: Yes."

At this point the court took a short recess. Gentry's testimony resumed later.

"Mr. Steinke: Mr. Gentry, we were talking just before the break about Leo Shively, Sharon Halstead's son. In the summer and early fall of 1988 when this was going on, how old was Leo?

"Mr. Gentry: Eight.

"Q: Was there something about his demeanor that gave these threats and his authority some credibility?

"A: Very serious look on his face. It was a look that said I'm not fooling around.

"Q: So that wasn't like an 8-year-old joking with an adult?

"A: No.

"Q: Did Leo use this claimed ability to see and hear God to his advantage?

"A: Yes.

"Q: Would it be fair to say that he was taking over control of things?

"A: In the family. He was the only person that could see and hear at the time.

"Q: Were there some incidents involving nighttime skateboarding that you recall?

"A: Yes.

"Q: Specifically what do you recall about that?

"A: It seemed odd that he would skateboard in the dark. I mentioned something and they said they would skateboard in the shopping plaza parking lot in Rogue River where it's lit up.

"Q: Was this something Leo insisted on doing?

"A: . . . God had told them it was all right to exercise by skateboarding at that time of night.

"Q: What about going to school? Did Leo receive any messages about going to school or staying out of school?

"A: Yes.

"Q: What were those?

"A: It started by not wanting to go to school, and he was actually cutting school for the day, but it led to a belief that Sharon could teach better at home the will of God, and [he] wouldn't learn all the unnecessary things that man teaches in the school.

"Q: When Leo told his mother that he had to go skateboarding at night in Rogue River, what did she do?

"A: I suppose she took them. I didn't go with them in the car.

"Q: Did she in fact take Leo out of school that fall?

"A: I believe so.

"Q: Was Leo also directing the family to engage in illegal activities, for example, stealing things?

"A: He wouldn't talk about stealing in front of me, but I questioned him on how he could receive a $140 skateboard when we were on welfare, and brand-new bicycle parts. He would say that he had just traded some kid for toys and that's how he received them.

"Q: Later on were there justifications that it was OK to steal from Satan or satanic people?

"A: Yes.

"Q: Can you tell the court in your own words what you were told about that?

"A: Satan has been governing the world for a long time, and we work all our lives, and at the end of our lives when it's retirement time we don't have very much because Satan is basically skimming off the top the stuff that we should have. Now, if you are a satanic person you are completely controlled and that gets wealth to him, and it would be justly right for a religious person that's doing the will of God to take this from you and use it for yourself, or give to the needy, somebody that needed it.

"Q: Did the members of the family believe that?

"A: I believe we were all in unison in the way we believed.

"Q: Did Leo ever indicate that he believed that he deserved to prosper because he could see and hear?

"A: He didn't say it outright in those words, but he told me what he was going to receive.

"Q: What did he say?

"A: His own room, his own motorcycle, and specific toys. A bow and arrow, and one of the boomerangs. Toys that a kid would like to have he was going to receive . . . after Sharon married Sam.

"Q: Did Leo claim an ability to be able to tell which people [belonged to] his God and which people [belonged to] Satan?

"A: Yes.

"Q: How did he claim to be able to do that?

"A: He could physically look at you as I see you now, and if he saw the light from the throne of God around you, emanating away from you, you were of God. But if he looked at a person that was so-called devil-controlled or was a satanist, there was darkness and a void of light and everything that this person was around was dark. Unfortunately, he also had the ability to see that not only in people but in their possessions that they owned.

"Q: If he saw that in someone's possessions, was it acceptable then to damage those possessions?

"A: Yes.

"Q: Can you recall any specific examples of that?

"A: Taking a knife to the whitewalls of tires. The owners of the cars were supposedly crooks, so it seemed perfectly logical to be able to flatten their tires, for a crook won't turn a crook in. Nothing would be said.

"Q: Did the family actually do this, go out and flatten tires?

"A: They told me they did.

"Q: Are you aware of an incident involving a neighbor lady who had a little dog?

"A: Several incidents.

"Q: Would you describe those or one that comes to your mind in your own words?

"A: The biggest one. The neighbor lady had a dog named Peewee. Supposedly while Sharon and I were in the house the kids were outside playing. The neighbor on the other side of the house moved away, and Harry and Leo happened to go into a vacant house and took a bottle of mustard out of the refrigerator and squeezed it at things. A squeezable mustard. They happened to go down the sidewalk squeezing the mustard on things when they hit the neighbor lady's car. And they didn't know that the mustard [would discolor] the paint job on the car. And [that would cause] the neighbors to phone the police on the kids.

"Q: Did Leo also tell the family that if somebody was possessed by Satan . . . it was all right to do physical injury to that person?

"A: It was all right to knock them out, unconscious.

"Q: In what context did that take place?

"A: I don't follow you.

"Q: Was there ever an incident in the park that you recall?

"A: Yes. We went to the park, because Leo was told that there was going to be a drug deal at Riverside. The drug dealers had a lot of money out, and we'd be taking it from them. So I drive them there. But they can't make up their mind who these drug dealers are. So while they're kind of bickering to themselves about it, I go to use the restroom, and when I come out they're all on the side of the sloping hill in the Riverside Park, and it's dark out, and I hear somebody scream, so I laughed because I knew Harry and Leo were frightening [somebody], so I keep walking toward them and I realize that something's out of control. Sharon and her sister, Harry, and Leo were standing around two people, and when I got there it made things look worse because I was such a big person that the people that were in the center of the ring were really sweating it out. They [Sharon and her sister and the children] wanted the money from these people, and supposedly they had no money on them, and the girl started crying, and the boy walked out of the circle and started running away, and so Debbie said well, let them go. They ran over to a car that had lots of other teenagers in it, but we all ran to my—we all ran to the car and I drove the car away without the headlights on so they could not see that we had left.

"Q: Was there ever a situation in which Leo directed the members of the family to go to Canada?

"A: Leo had convinced Sharon, and after Sharon realized it was God's invention she convinced me, and I drove them up to Canada.

"Q: What was the purpose of the trip to Canada?

"A: To talk to a minister of the church about what we were doing in Grants Pass.

"Q: Did you speak to that minister?

"A: We spoke to him, but he was highly upset because arson had just burnt his church down the same week, and he did not say what he was supposed to say to us, so we got kind of aggravated and we left Canada.

"Q: Whose car did you drive up there?

"A: Blue Pinto.

"Q: Whose car was that at the time?

"A: I don't recall. It was either Sharon's—I believe it was Sharon's at the time.

"Q: Did she later sign that over to you?

"A: Yes.

"Q: Was that because of a prediction of her impending marriage?

"A: That, and I could insure the car.

"Q: Did you ever try to warn Sharon about what was going on with Leo?

"A: Yes.

"Q: What was her reaction?

"A: She was annoyed, and then she tried to explain to me that I was wrong and I could not interfere with God and His plans for us, as we were God's little soldiers.

"Q: Do you know what it means to be totaled?

"A: Yes.

"Q: What does that mean to you in your own words?

"A: A satanist. A man that would believe that Satan is as strong as God, and they prefer to follow Satan [rather] than God.

"Q: Did you know what it means to go backward through the doors and becoming totaled?

"A: Yes.

"Q: In your own words describe what that is.

"A: That would be to knowingly do something against the laws of God and break them deliberately and slip from the standard of God that is in His eyes good, slowly regressing backward until finally you had no more love for your fellow man in you and you cared only about yourself.

"Q: Do you know how many doors there are until you're totaled?

"A: Seven, but you get through four of them and you've gone too far.

"Q: Did Leo ever tell you that you had gone four doors backward?

"A: Yes.

"Q: When was that?

"A: It was in the middle of the year of '88. He told me I had one chance to cast these satanic agencies out of myself or there would be no point in me seeing them anymore.

"Q: Did Deborah tell you how to cast the demons out?

"A: She mentioned a few things, but I told her I already knew how to do it.

"Q: Did you actually do something to try to cast the demons out or to appease the family?

"A: Yes.

"Q: What specifically did you do?

"A: It was something that I was going to try to avoid, because they told me that when I did it, most likely I would be killed when the brakes on my car would go out, or I would drive over the edge of the road. I was to drive up in the mountains and ask for the angels of God to escort all the demonic angels around me and the car to the never-ending pit. So I went up in the mountains and I prayed, and then I left.

"Mr. Steinke: Thank you. That's all I have."

"Mr. Frasier: Mr. Gentry, as I understand it, at one point in time you were Sharon's at-times live-in boyfriend; is that correct?

"Mr. Gentry: Yes.

"Q: How long did you actually live with the defendant?

"A: To be living in the house with her full-time was about three years.

"Q: What is the current status of your relationship with the defendant?

"A: Well, she's locked up, and I believe she's either in Portland or in Grants Pass.

"Q: I want to ask you this, Mr. Gentry: do you still love the defendant?

"A: Yes.

"Q: Mr. Gentry, you have indicated that you have had several opportunities to go over to the residence of Dave and Lynn Greene; is that correct?

"A: Yes.

"Q: You have been over there numerous times?

"A: Yes.

"Q: Wouldn't you agree that Dave and Lynn Greene were a kind, loving couple?

"A: Yes.

"Q: Good parents?

"A: Yes.

"Q: Nice family?

"A: Yes.

"Q: Now, Sharon and you started going to this group in Canyonville around 1983, 1984; is that correct?

"A: Yes.

"Q: Sharon's sister also came at that time, that's Deborah?

"A: Yes.

"Q: Then she subsequently moved to California in 1984; is that correct?

"A: Yes.

"Q: Now, so when you were going over to Dave and Lynn Greene's house, that's with yourself and Sharon, Deborah Halstead's not involved with that at all; is that correct?

"A: I recall testifying there.

"Q: Do you recall being asked by myself at the grand jury if they, meaning Sharon and Deborah, threatened you physically or made any threats toward you? Do you recall that question I asked you in the grand jury?

"A: Yes.

"Q: Do you remember how you responded to that question?

"A: I believe I told you about Debbie. Wherever Debbie goes, Sharon follows.

"Q: Do you remember your response as being 'Yes, they said that they were tired of listening to my demons' and 'that it was time I be taken out'?

"A: Yes.

"Q: Do you remember saying that? Isn't it true that Sharon participated in threatening you?

"A: She was only standing beside her sister.

"Q: Isn't it because of this threat you moved out of the residence?

"A: Yes.

"Q: Did Sharon ever tell you that 'we had to take out Satan's people'?

"A: Yes.

"Q: How did you respond to that, Mr. Gentry?

"A: She referred to it in the future. There would be two classes of people. There was good and bad. And I just thought to myself, *Until that time comes I won't worry about it.*

"Q: Isn't it true, Mr. Gentry, that you told Sharon Halstead that 'that's for God to do—you don't take them out'?

"A: Yes.

"Q: And you told her that prior to any of the killings that have occurred?

"A: Yes.

"Q: Were you asked by Sharon to kill someone?

"A: She strongly suggested that I defend myself against her ex-husband.

"Q: What do you mean by that, sir?

"A: He has a weak heart, and he wouldn't be able to take being hit in the chest.

"Q: So you described to her how you could kill Mr. Tex Shively by striking him in the chest?

"A: I didn't describe it to her. She knows I could only because of the karate training I had in the past.

"Q: Did the defendant ever seek advice from you on how to kill someone and perhaps conceal the body?

"A: Yes.

"Q: Would you describe that for us, please?

"A: I had taken the family out to see a movie. It was a Rambo show, and after the show I suggested that that was a poor way of hurting people the way he did it, [that] it would be best to make it look like an accident. I would give him a little extra shove over the side of Hellgate Canyon. She said something about the ability to be able to recognize a person if he did that, and I just thought to myself, *Why wouldn't you want to be able to recognize them?* And in such a way she talked to me, I kind of told her a way in which you could kill a person and [discard] body parts, making it unable for the police to identify the body by taking out the handprint and all dental work, and maybe [discarding] it into the woods in let's say another county.

"Q: Mr. Gentry, you have testified here today that Leo was giving some direction to the defendant, and some of the things that he was saying was that things should be stolen; is that correct?

"A: That Leo?

"Q: Leo.

"A: Yes, just Leo.

"Q: Leo was saying they should go and steal stuff?

"A: Specific things.

"Q: Did you ever go and steal anything at the direction of Leo?

"A: No.

"Q: Did you ever slash any tires at the direction of Leo?

"A: No.

"Q: Did you ever assault any person at the direction of Leo?

"A: Never.

"Q: Why?

"A: They wouldn't invite me. They realized that the way I believed my religious walk with God was a little different than theirs. And I knew that I would put up a real fuss, and I know that Debbie Halstead didn't want me to be around the . . . family.

"Q: Did you believe that Leo was hearing from an angel of God?

"A: I thought that he was at first. But after I heard the things, the messages that he received, I knew he was just making it up.

"Q: So in other words, you saw through what you perceived as a ruse on the part of Leo Halstead?

"A: Yes.

"Q: After the defendant was arrested, did you ever visit her in jail?

"A: Yes.

"Q: Did you ever inquire of her if the authorities would ever know the truth of what occurred?

"A: Did I ask her that?

"Q: Did you have a conversation along the line if the authorities would ever find out the truth?

"A: Kind of.

"Q: Do you know what the defendant said, or do you recall what she said?

"A: She made it kind of specific that nobody would ever know.

"Q: She stated that they will never know the truth?

"A: Yes.

"Mr. Frasier: Thank you. I have nothing further."

"Mr. Steinke: Mr. Gentry, you say that after a time you did not believe that Leo could see and hear God; is that right?

"Mr. Gentry: Right.

"Q: Did Sharon believe that Leo could see and hear God?

"A: She always did.

"Mr. Steinke: Thank you. That's all we have of this witness, Your Honor.

"Mr. Frasier: Nothing further.

"The Court: You may step down" (Circuit Court of the State of Oregon, court transcripts, vol. 101).

CHAPTER FOURTEEN

SURPRISED, AMAZED, AND SHOCKED

W hen I first was arrested and put in jail I was in shock," Sharon Lee told me. "In everything I had done I had believed I was doing the Lord's will. And I couldn't understand why God was allowing me to be put in jail."

During the time that I interviewed Sharon and Deborah in Salem, Oregon, the prison authorities would not allow me to bring any paper or pen to make notes of any kind. So I asked the sisters to write down certain parts of their experiences and mail them to me. Then as I wrote this book I could use some of their very own words to give greater accuracy to my work. Much of the material quoted here comes from their letters to me.

"In February of 1984 Lynn Greene, because of her prophetic gift, was given a message from the Lord Jesus," Sharon Lee said, "that both my sister and I were being given each a companion angel to help us in our Christian walk. They came directly from the throne of God at a very stressful time when we needed heavenly help. Deborah received her companion angel a few hours before me. According to Lynn, Jesus had commissioned these angels to stay with us and be our companions and friends. They would never leave our sides unless we asked them to.

"Sometimes on Sabbath we would ask them if they would like to go back to heaven for a visit. They would say yes, that they wanted to sit at the feet of Jesus and enjoy His presence. When they supposedly came back from being with Jesus and the other heavenly angels, they said they always felt refreshed, but wanted to come back to be with us. They always returned with encouraging words from Jesus, and many times brought us spiritual gifts. These spiritual gifts Lynn could see, and she would tell us about them. I must say that I named my angel Sam.

"Again," Sharon said, "when doing the missions the angels directed us to do, we knew we had their help and support. At the end of our commissions, which we believed were from God, I knew I wouldn't be able to do or accomplish anything without an angel's help. So when it was time for me to destroy the physical bodies of the persons the angels said God had taken their spirits to heaven, I asked my companion angel to stand in my body and help me do the Lord's will. I knew I couldn't have done what I did without my angel's help.

"Several times after having been told to destroy certain individuals," Sharon wrote, "I questioned whether I would be doing right, and my companion angel, Sam, would say that Satan was working on me to stop me from doing the Lord's will. I believed what he said. Besides, such bright and beautiful beings had to come from God, so I did what I believed to be His will, and shot people."

The Halsteads' experience, besides showing how easy it is to fall into error and deception, raised a number of issues that each of us must wrestle with as we seek truth. How far do we dare go in the pursuit of truth? Besides theological issues, what ethical and other criteria must we always keep in mind? Judge Gerald C. Neufeld alluded to some of them during the sentencing hearing, recorded below. Their story raises questions that we must ask ourselves when confronted with something that claims to be truth and demands our allegiance.

"The Court: First of all, I'd like to make some comments by way of a general nature concerning the presentation of this case over the last several months, and the only comment I would make in that regard is that I'd like to thank counsel, and that is counsel for both the state and the defense, for the professional and competent way that they have dealt with each other and the court in this case. It makes, I think, everyone's job easier if there is an

air of professionalism and certainly competent counsel for everyone to deal with, and I appreciate all of your efforts in that regard.

"The second thing I'd like to say is by the very subject matter we're dealing with, the court's going to be required to make
some comment on religious beliefs, and it is certainly not my intention to degrade or in any way put down people who hold religious beliefs similar with those that have been discussed here. It's
simply in the nature of analyzing this case there is going to have
to be some comments made on the religious aspects of it.

"This is really about the only time a judge gets to speak
probably about his thoughts on a particular case. The way our system is set up is that once a defendant enters a plea, then the court
is given certain information, either through agreement of the par-
ties or by way of a presentence investigation. Testimony as has
been heard in this case can be presented, and in a large number of
cases it is not presented, and then the court decides what sentence
would be appropriate.

"In this particular case counsel has supplied the court with a
great deal of information about this case. I have been supplied
with the entire transcript, some 156 pages of Deborah Halstead's
statement. I was given a seven-and-a-half-to-eight-page stipula-
tion as to what the facts of this case were. And contained in that,
of course, is information concerning the respective positions of
what each party feels would be an appropriate sentence.

"Contrary to what a lot of people might think, the court
really does not have a real intimate knowledge of the facts of this
case. Much of what I know about this case I've learned for the very
first time in the last week or two as I began to get this information. And I think there's a good reason for that. I think that if the
court early on is given intimate knowledge of the facts, the open
mind that I think a judge must have in situations like this can very
easily be skewed in one direction or the other. So the information
that I am relying upon is what I do know about this case, what has
been presented to me in the last day and a half, and again, the
abundance of information that counsel has supplied to me.

"I think one of the things that a case like this does is it makes you go back, because the stakes are so high, go back to the fundamentals of what sentencing is really all about. Without any questions, sentencing is easily the most difficult and probably the most controversial thing a judge does. We only have to read the newspaper about sentences that are handed down by courts, and in many instances people in the general public feel very strongly about those sentences. And so it's been helpful to me in the sense that I think it makes me go back and really analyze what we are doing with sentencing and what the law of sentencing is.

"Probably the most fundamental recitation of what sentencing is all about is contained in the Oregon Constitution. Article 1, Section 15, says that laws for the punishment of crime shall be founded on principles of reformation and not on vindictive justice. The section that follows that, which is Section 16, among other things says that cruel and unusual punishment shall not be inflicted, but all penalties shall be in proportion to the offense.

"There have been many, many cases, some of which actually tested the death penalty in this state, brought under those respective sections, and case law has interpreted those sections to mean, at least in the context that we're using them here, and I'm going to cite out of a fairly typical case, *State v. Thornton,* 244 Oregon 104, this is the Oregon Supreme Court, we have often said that where no improper motives can be attached to the action of the trial court we should not modify the sentence unless it was so disproportionate to the offense as to shock the conscience of fair-minded men.

"So the test is really a two-part test. One is whether or not the court has some improper motive and is engaging in vindictive justice, and second, does the sentence the court hands down, is it proportionate to the offense, or does it shock the conscience of fair-minded men?

"I think there are three things the court under that scheme, that very basic scheme, is required to look at, and I think that is the court must look at the crime itself, the court is required to look at the defendant as an individual person and the things that she brings to this sentencing, and third, I think under somewhat recent legislation compared to some of these other things, the court I think is required to say something about the impact that this has had on the victims in this case.

"I'm not going to spend a lot of time rehashing the facts. Everyone has heard those facts. Suffice it to say that the events that occurred here, and you can use a lot of different words, a travesty, a tragedy, any word like that, that comes to your mind, and I suppose in trying to analyze this case initially it was difficult to get a handle on why this whole series of events happened. The case has been characterized as bizarre, but I guess what I would ask [is] Is it really bizarre?

"I've come to the conclusion that what we have here, and it's common knowledge, as a result of certain religious beliefs that the defendant held, together with whatever influence her son Leo may have had over her, that the Greene family had to be destroyed. That is the real driving thought behind the whole series of events that occurred here, and the question is How responsible are people to be held for acting on the beliefs they sincerely hold, yet under any sort of reasonable standard those beliefs are both dangerous and erroneous?

"I would submit that this case is really not a bizarre case, but rather, it is in a lot of ways very typical of what we see in a lot of reprehensible criminal behavior. I don't know how many presentence investigations I've read. I've read one in this case, and probably 80 to 90 percent of the sentencings a judge does he has a presentence investigation, and in that we always are able to find some reason generally for why certain behavior occurs. What distinguishes this case from perhaps other cases, most other cases, is the fact that it is religious beliefs that are driving the conduct as opposed to things like drugs, alcohol, mental disease, or things like extreme emotional disturbance, that the law recognizes. We see those things as driving people's behavior in a lot of cases, and what we have here is just another kind of influence that's driving behavior, and that's what makes this case perhaps distinguishable . . . that what is driving it is not what we are used to, it is not the conventional things that are driving behavior, it's a set of religious beliefs.

"While the influence of religious beliefs may help us understand the criminal behavior in this case, in my opinion it is of little assistance in assessing responsibility. If we had a system that allowed people to be exonerated or their behavior minimized because of sincerely held beliefs, then travesties such as Nazi Germany would be allowed to exist. That's exactly what happened. The Nazi German people believed the Jewish race was an inferior, non-Aryan race, and we saw 6 million people later the results of that. Those beliefs were sincerely held by some people. That's an extreme example, but that's really what we're talking about here.

"Responsibility and accountability must be there for all of us, despite the fact that we may hold beliefs that justify breaking the law. I think the quote that perhaps sums this case up better than any I was able to find is contained on the very last page of Deborah Halstead's statement, because I think it points out a lot of things. It points out perhaps the lack of remorse, the lack of I think real appreciation for what was really done to the Greene family, and I'm just going to read a portion of it to you.

"This is an attorney questioning Deborah Halstead:

" 'OK, and then the final and third point I want to ask about is the only reason why Dave Greene, Lynn Greene, and Nathaniel Greene were shot was because they were totaled?' Miss Halstead's answer was 'Yes.' Attorney: 'And they were not shot to try to cover up or prevent in some way you and Sharon from using any credit cards?' Answer: 'Of course not.' The attorney then said, 'All right, that's all I have.' And then Miss Halstead interjected, 'That would be stupid.'

"A clear implication from that statement is that there is very little appreciation for the seriousness of what happened here, and that while it would have been stupid . . . to try and kill these people because they were thinking about using their credit cards, it wasn't stupid to try and kill them for what went on here. And I think that statement sums this case up, at least a large number of the elements of the case.

"Turning to the defendant herself, she's going to be 37 years

176

of age in November of this year. In reading the presentence report—I've never had an opportunity to talk to her—she apparently had a very difficult childhood. She has no prior criminal history that anybody has been able to determine. She's had very spotty employment, and she's been diagnosed by Dr. Jantser as having a 'dependency personality disorder.'

"In addition, she comes to this court as having already been sentenced to 30 years for an aggravated murder that occurred in Yamhill County, and of course, that in a lot of ways does have a substantial impact on what this court has available to it in the way of perhaps sentencing alternatives.

"I would agree with Mr. Frasier that Dr. Jantser's report is void of any discussion of treatability of this dependency personality disorder, especially as treatment may have to occur—well, it will have to occur—in the confines of prison.

"The report also does not address whether the defendant could be dangerous now or at some point in the future. I think the court should in terms of the very first thing I read, the principles of reformation, I think the court should and I'm going to assess whether I believe this personality disorder is severe or not. I think the relevance of that inquiry is that if one commits dangerous crimes such as this one because of a—at least partially because of a severe personality disorder, then it can be persuasively argued that they are less amenable to reformation or rehabilitation.

"Essentially what I've heard here for the last day and a half, and what I've read in this transcript, is there are basically two conclusions one can come to as to the level that she was under the influence of her son's control or these religious beliefs that she was entertaining at the time. The first conclusion is that those beliefs and her son [are] being used as a scapegoat to explain and minimize her culpability in this set of events. Or that in fact these things did occur and that there was some sort of role reversal in terms of her being in control of her children, where her children became in control of her.

"I read this entire transcript, and I guess certainly it would be an argument that could be made that it's very difficult for me to believe that a boy as young as Leo, who was 8 or 9 years of age, could conceptualize, even a very bright boy, as he has been described, can conceptualize some of the things that are talked about in this statement of Deborah Halstead's.

"In addition to that, there's been more than ample evidence here that the defendant was aware of her son's behavior problems at school, even took steps to try and deal with those, but despite being aware of those and despite trying to deal with those, decided to go ahead and let her sons control her, so I think there is a good argument that can be made that at least in some part this 8- or 9-year-old's ability to control his mother and I guess two grown adults' behavior to the extent that he was able to is certainly suspect.

"However, giving the defendant the benefit of the doubt that this role reversal did occur, . . . I think any reasonable standard would have to tell you that this personality disorder, if that is in fact what contributed to this event here, or these events, . . . would have to be characterized as severe, and we have a total loss of parental control, engaging in antisocial behavior that is of the highest proportions . . . And given the fact that she is going to be locked up for the next 30 years at the very least, and knowing what I know about the ability to get the kind of one-on-one counseling and other kinds of counseling necessary to treat severe personality disorders like this, I would say that I have real concerns as to whether this defendant is treatable or not, given the environment that she is going to be in. And I would say the chances are very good that she is not going to be treated to the extent that is going to be necessary to deal with this problem.

"I think given the case then, . . . I would have to conclude that if she is not treatable, then . . . the chances of rehabilitation are very small, but of course, any sentencing the court participates in, one has to assess the likelihood of rehabilitation, and of course, the less likely it is, I believe the more justification there is for incarceration and lengthy terms of incarceration.

"The final thing that I think the court is required to look at is the impact on the victims here, and I don't think I need to repeat what was obviously a very emotional display by Mr. Greene and Mrs. Sapienzae [Lynn Greene's mother] on how this whole series of events has impacted them. Within a matter of seconds and minutes this entire family has had its life—had their lives—turned upside down, decimated and . . . permanently changed. Nathaniel's life has been permanently changed. Mr. Greene isn't going to be able to experience the kind of things that he would have been able to experience with both his wife and his son. He is going to have the responsibility for the rest of his life to look after his son. There has been a substantial impact on each victim, and I think that certainly should play some consideration in the court's sentence.

"The sentence the court can impose in this case is far more discretionary than the one Judge Blensley in McMinnville could impose. His sentence was pretty much dictated by statute.

"The primary discretion that I have in this case is whether or not to make the sentence consecutive, and what minimums, if any, the court should impose. In my opinion, consecutive sentences and minimums are reserved for those individuals whose conduct and presence present the greatest danger to society. Every statutory scheme that allows the court that kind of discretion to provide for an enhanced penalty has as a component considerations that relate to danger, the type of behavior that was involved, and the protection of society. That principle is most legally supported when you're dealing with crimes against persons as opposed to crimes against property, such as what we have here.

"ORS 137.123 sets forth the legal principles the court must use in the facts that have been presented here. I think everyone has conceded here that we do have a situation where we have more than one criminal offense arising out of a continuous and uninterrupted course of conduct. And that being the case, if the court is going to impose consecutive sentences, the court has to make the following findings:

"The court has discretion to impose consecutive terms of imprisonment for separate convictions arising out of a continuous and uninterrupted course of conduct only if the court finds (a) that the criminal offense for which a consecutive sentence is contemplated was not merely an incidental violation of a separate statutory provision in the course of the commission of a more serious crime, but rather was an indication of defendant's willingness to commit more than one criminal offense. Or (and the court can find either one of these) (b) the criminal offense for which a consecutive sentence is contemplated caused or created a risk of causing greater or qualitatively different loss, injury or harm to the victim or caused or created a risk of causing loss, injury, or harm to a different victim than was caused or threatened by the other offense or offenses committed during a continuous and uninterrupted course or conduct.

"In my review of the facts and of the evidence heard here in the last day and a half, I would conclude that the facts of this case support the court finding that both of these exist, not just one of them. Clearly the act of trying to kill or attempting to kill the three victims in the Greenes' house were more than mere incidental conduct, and [when] I think of incidental conduct, I think of conduct of someone breaking into somebody's house and on the way out taking a bottle or something and throwing it through the window. That to me would be incidental conduct. This reaches far beyond that.

"In addition, clearly the risk, the actual risk, this isn't the creation of a risk, this is risk that actually occurred by which subsection (b), that to Mr. Greene and Nathaniel, given the facts of this case, caused additional loss and injury to those individuals.

"The court would make a finding that despite the fact that we have uninterrupted conduct here, . . . the criteria that would allow the court to impose consecutive sentences in these cases does exist.

"Dealing with count number seven first, which is the charge of murder with a firearm, the court is required by law to sentence the defendant to the physical and legal control of the corrections division, for a period of her natural life.

"The issue before the court is whether the court ought to impose a 10-year minimum sentence as is required by statute, or whether the court may add an additional 15 years without the possibility of parole, release or work release, or any form of temporary leave or employment at a forest or work camp. In my judgment, this is a case, given the gravity of the impact that it has had on people, [in which] I'm going to make a finding that I believe the court should—this is a more aggravated situation, and I have sentenced a number of murder defendants in this court, and I would say perhaps with one exception this is probably the most grievous set of facts that I have ever come across, and I feel that it is deserving of more than the 10-year minimum, and I'm going to impose a 15-year minimum that the statute, 163.115, subsection 3, subsection (C), allows. The court will make that sentence consecutive to any other sentence the court is going to impose here today and consecutive to the sentence that was imposed in Yamhill County.

"Count number eight, attempted murder of David Greene, Jr., the court will sentence the defendant to 20 years in the penitentiary, with a mandatory minimum sentence of 10 years, consecutive to any other sentence, consecutive to the Yamhill sentence.

"Count nine, which is the attempted murder of Nathaniel Greene, the court will sentence the defendant to 20 years with a 10-year minimum sentence, consecutive to any other sentence the court has imposed, consecutive to the Yamhill sentence. As part of that 10-year minimum the court under 161.610 will impose the five-year gun enhancement. 161.610, subsection 3, says if a defendant is convicted of a felony having as an element the defendant's use or threatened use of a firearm during the commission of the crime, the court shall impose at least a minimum term of imprisonment as provided in subsection 4, except as provided in subsection 5. Subsection 5 is [that] the court would expressly have to find mitigating circumstances such to sentence the defendant to a lesser sentence, and I specifically do not find in this set of facts any mitigation that would justify the court not imposing the firearm enhancement.

"In addition, the court has been asked and the court will address the issue as to whether or not there was significant planning or preparation involved in this case. And the court would incorporate as its findings in this case, and I am going to make that finding, pages 10 and 11 of plaintiff's trial memorandum or sentencing memorandum, and specifically items 1 through 9. Those include the following:

"(1) that the defendant assisted her son, Leo, in obtaining the gun that was used in the murder. She took him to his father's home with the knowledge that he was going to steal a gun.

"(2) the defendant took possession of the gun from her son after it had been stolen.

"(3) the defendant test-fired the gun prior to the shooting.

"(4) the defendant was aware of and used ammunition stolen by her sister in both murders.

"(5) the defendant was aware that the Greenes would have to be killed based on Leo's assertion that they were totaled.

"(6) the defendant discussed the fact that the Greene family would be killed and how they would be taken elsewhere to be killed other than doing the actual murder in the Greene family residence.

"(7) the defendant helped or was present when restraints were obtained in the form of toy handcuffs from a local Payless store immediately prior to the murder of Lynn Greene.

"(8) the defendant went to the Greene home with the express intent to kill the whole family. She brought with her the gun . . . used in the killing and the attempted murders, and sufficient ammunition was also brought in the truck to reload the gun, and

"(9) finally, at the direction of her son, she completed the plan by shooting the Greene family and she did her best to kill all three, in that she shot David Greene in the back as he fled seeking help, shot Lynn Greene at extremely close range, and shot Nathaniel in the face.

"In addition to those things, the court would incorporate . . . State's Exhibit 18, pages 91 through 96, which is a recitation of the statement by Deborah Halstead of the events leading up to and including the incident at the Greenes' home.

"And finally, as a further finding the court would find that Deborah Halstead has pled guilty to the charge of conspiracy to commit murder, and that district attorney's information alleges that on or about November 4, 1988, in Josephine County, Oregon, she did unlawfully with the intent that conduct constituting the crime of murder, punishable as a felony, be performed, agree with Sharon Halstead to engage in and cause the performance of the following conduct to unlawfully and intentionally cause the death of other human beings, to wit, Lynn Greene, Nathaniel Greene, and David Greene, by shooting the said victims with a firearm. Legally, conspiracy contemplates the making of an agreement, and in my opinion, it also constitutes some evidence of planning and significant preparation.

"I would direct that the state make those findings. They will be made a part of the judgment order in the case. The final thing I'm going to say is that I think, Miss Halstead, through the competence of not only your attorneys but all of the people that worked for you in this case . . . those people on your behalf were able to convince the state of Oregon to spare your life, and I think that society would be justifiably outraged if this court did anything but make sure to the best of its ability . . . that you don't as a part of that life also have one other day of freedom for the acts that you committed here.

"Mr. Hadley, would you advise the defendant of her right to appeal from the court's sentence?

"Mr. Hadley: I will do that, Your Honor.

"Mr. Frasier: Your Honor, I have prepared the findings of fact that the court spoke of. I've already shown this to Mr. Hadley, and I tender it to the court at this time, and I also have a motion to dismiss the balance of the indictment. I hand those to the court.

"The Court: The court will be in recess.

"Mr. Frasier: Your Honor, could I ask a point of clarification? On the murder charge, I believe you mentioned a 15-year minimum. Was it the court's intent to make it a total of 25 years?

"The Court: I meant to make it a total of 25. The 15 was in addition to the 10.

"Mr. Frasier: Thank you" (Circuit Court of the State of Oregon, court transcripts, vol. 101).

Newspaper coverage was again extensive.

"The sentencing hearing for Sharon Halstead started this morning with emotional testimony. . . .

"[David] Greene [Jr.] occasionally broke down and wept. . . .

"Greene told the judge of crying for three months over the loss of 'someone you have loved, who you have held hands with and have always wanted.' The memory of his wife's screams as she was killed will echo in his mind for the rest of his life, he said.

"As for his son, 'he will never have the freedom to live normally again.' Greene wiped his eyes as he told of his son's tricycle standing idle and his sandbox filled with weeds.

" 'Only Nathaniel knows what it is like to lie in bed 45 days . . . and not be able to speak. . . .'

"Sgt. Verlin David testified about finding notebooks with religious writings in Halstead's home after the murder. They were similar to material found in the Greene home, the detective said" (Grants Pass *Daily Courier,* Sept. 26, 1989).

"Testimony about the group . . . concluded in the case this morning . . .

"According to the testimony . . . Halstead joined a Bible group with several other members of the Grants Pass Seventh-day Adventist Church, including her friends David and Lynn Greene . . . Another [group] member was John Gentry. He later became Halstead's live-in boyfriend. . . .

"Witnesses testified . . . today that the group gradually shifted from studying the Bible to spiritualism. . . .

"The [religious] group became aware of another one . . . led by Jean Ketzner, who supposedly had the ability to cast out devils and speak directly to God.

"Members of the study group attended several sessions in which Ketzner performed exorcisms. . . . Seventh-day Adventist [Church] official Larry Evans later described the splinter group as deliverance ministries" *(ibid.,* Sept. 27, 1989).

Surprised, Amazed, and Shocked

"GRANTS PASS—The husband of Lynnann Greene, a murder victim, testified Tuesday that his son still asks for his dead mother and that his wife's death 'should be met with death.'

"David Greene testified during the . . . sentencing hearing for Sharon Halstead, who has pleaded guilty to the Nov. 5, 1988, fatal shooting of the 32-year-old teacher. David Greene and his son were wounded in the incident.

"The shooting left the boy, Nathaniel Greene, 3, paralyzed from the chest down. David Greene, who later recovered, told the court how the killing affected him and his son. Also testifying was Lynn Greene's mother, Antonette Sapienzae.

"Other evidence submitted to the court included a videotape of the Greenes' home where the shooting occurred and religious writings from Halstead's Grants Pass home. Also entered into evidence was a taped interview in which David Greene described how [Sharon] Halstead and her sister, Deborah, participated in prayer groups with the Greenes and others in which all discussed hearing messages from God and angels.

"According to early court documents, Sharon's then 9-year-old son, Leo, had directed the shootings, claiming that he had messages from God saying that the victims were possessed by demons.

"In his statement to the court, David Greene talked about his paralyzed son and how he had to listen to his boy telling him, 'I want my mommy.' Greene talked about what it was like to 'rip up the carpet and see the blood of someone you loved. . . .'

"The hearing is expected to continue Wednesday. Deborah Halstead was previously sentenced for conspiracy to commit murder. Sharon Halstead was sentenced earlier in Yamhill County for aggravated murder of Newberg ranch hand Mike Lemke. He was killed two days before Lynnann Greene was shot and killed" (Portland *Oregonian,* Sept. 27, 1989).

"Saying it would be an outrage if murderer Sharon Halstead were ever allowed another day of freedom, Judge Gerald Neufeld [on] Wednesday handed her the maximum prison terms possible.

"He sentenced her to life in prison with a 25-year minimum

for murder . . . two 20-year prison terms with 10-year minimums for two counts of attempted murder and . . . another five years because she used a gun.

"Neufeld ordered all of the sentences, with the exception of the gun penalty, be served consecutively. He also ordered they be served consecutively with a 30-year minimum sentence she has already received in a Yamhill County aggravated murder case.

"According to prosecutors, the 75 years of minimum sentences should ensure Halstead never leaves prison alive. . . .

"Neufeld said Halstead's case was different from all others he has seen because the driving force behind the crimes was her religious beliefs. Halstead believed her 9-year-old son, Leo, when he told her God said the Greenes had to be killed because they were possessed by demons.

"While this explanation helped with understanding why [Sharon] Halstead shot the family, it wasn't of much assistance in assessing responsibility, the judge said.

"If society reduced punishment because of sincere beliefs, 'then travesties such as Nazi Germany could be allowed to exist,' the Josephine County Circuit Court judge said.

"In closing arguments, Deputy District Attorney Paul Frasier described what Halstead had done to the Greene family as unspeakable. . . .

"Freedom of religion doesn't give anyone the right to take another's life and didn't excuse Halstead's conduct, Frasier said.

"Defense attorney Kenneth Hadley told the judge the defense didn't offer an excuse for a justification for what Halstead had done, just an explanation. . . .

"According to testimony in the trial, Halstead and the Greenes all belonged to the Grants Pass Seventh-day Adventist Church. They also were members of a prayer group that began studying the Bible about 1983. The direction of the group changed over the years, and by 1987 they were heavily involved in spiritualism. Group members believed they could hear and see messages from God and the angels.

"Their beliefs fell far outside the mainstream of accepted

Adventist theology, according to other testimony in the trial. . . .

"Deborah Halstead previously pleaded guilty to murder conspiracies in both counties and is serving a 20-year term in prison.

"The boys were never charged with a crime and are currently wards of the court. A Seventh-day Adventist agency helped the state children's services division find foster homes for the boys with members of the church, according to Jay Prall, director of communication of the Oregon Conference of Seventh-day Adventists. He said Leo is living with a family in which the wife is a counselor" (Grants Pass *Daily Courier,* Sept. 28, 1989).

IT'S TIME TO SAY THANK YOU

Sharon and Deborah Halstead greatly appreciate the help they received from a number of people during the first five years of their incarceration while they were regaining their faith in Christ's power to save and were establishing a new relationship with our heavenly Father. Their lives, I believe, disprove Judge Neufeld's fear that Sharon Halstead was beyond the possibility of reformation.

Space permits me to mention but a few of the individuals who helped them.

"When I was first arrested and put in jail," Sharon told me, "Pastor Steve Poenitz came to visit me in jail. He let me know that the Grants Pass Seventh-day Adventist Church was having me disfellowshiped. He took my phone calls and came to visit me regularly. I even became acquainted with his wife, Ernestine, and often talked with her over the phone. They both helped a great deal to keep my morale up, and let me know Jesus still loved me. Pastor Poenitz . . . helped with getting my head straightened around after the past five years of delusional beliefs."

Both sisters have told me of the help they received from Pastor Reginald Robinson during the first five years of their incarceration. During their stay in jail before their transfer to state prison, the two women seriously considered taking their own lives. Their mother prayed for help on what she could do to help them, then remembered that her daughters always enjoyed Elder Robinson's speaking, and contacted him at the Adventist Media Center. He flew up to see the sisters. During the following months he visited them numerous times, talked with them over the phone to bring them inspiration and guidance, and never got tired of assisting them.

I don't want to forget to mention Chaplain LeRoy Klein, who was another wonderful influence and Bible teacher. Every Monday evening for more than five years he gave them Bible studies at the Oregon Women's Correction Center. He was a mighty influence for good.

A SPECIAL THANKS

Both sisters have told me how thankful they are to their parents for "sticking by them" during the past eight years of their incarceration. They have regularly visited and encouraged their daughters in dealing with prison life. "My father," Sharon said, "always tells me that this was all in God's hands, and that He would see us through everything, and free us when the time was right. When most of my relatives turned their back on us, my parents stuck by us, and they still do."

And it is the hope of both Sharon and Deborah Halstead, as well as my hope, that the reader will learn from their experience of Satan's power to deceive even the most confident of us. Let us cling to His Holy Spirit so that we can see through his distortion and twisting of truth into dangerous error.

A P P E N D I X

After a year of researching and studying the case of the Halstead sisters, the day has arrived for me to ship the manuscript to the publishers. But before doing so, I wish to touch on what I believe has become an important point to my readers.

Many have been curious how I can recall in such great detail experiences that took place in my life 50 years ago when I was affiliated with spirit worshipers. To be honest with you, I must say that I can't do that unaided. But I can say with joy in my heart that I have received divine help when I have prayed for God's Holy Spirit to enable me to recall certain events as if they had occurred yesterday. Even after giving this type of answer, I have had a couple people say that they can't understand why God would do such a thing for me. Then, after helping them see things from another perspective by asking one simple question, they agreed with me that having a right relationship with one's God can be extremely beneficial.

Let me present that perspective by asking a question: *What do you think is the hardest for the Lord to do—to bring small details to my remembrance after 50 years, or to have His Holy Spirit create toner in my copier's toner cartridge daily for 741 days, a little more than two years in time?* (Read the story in chapter 1 of *When You Need Incredible Answers to Prayer.*) The print cartridge was rated for 1,200 copies, which it made. Then in answer to a prayer of need, the Spirit of God took over, and the machine produced more than 3,000 copies until I accidentally overheated the unit and caused a circuit board to catch fire, destroying the copier. But I have kept the copier as a monument similar to those God called for in the Bible to remind others of His love and grace and infinite goodness. God can keep an empty toner cartridge making copies, or He can bring back to mind forgotten memories. He will do whatever He sees as necessary for us, whether it be something spectacular or something simple and humble.

Deceptions in the last days

"I told God I would do anything for Him. But I never thought He would send an angel to tell me to destroy people. Firing those shots was the most difficult thing I had done to please Him."

—Sharon Lee Halstead

Sharon Lee was a devoted, fourth-generation Seventh-day Adventist. What horrifying events led her to become a killer for God? Roger Morneau reveals the tactics Satan used to entice members of her Bible study group into heresy, vandalism, robbery, and murder.

Beware of Angels is a chilling demonstration of how Satan can deceive even those armed with the truth.

Church leaders urged Roger Morneau to tell this story and use his unique understanding of the supernatural to help God's people avoid the satanic deceptions that even now threaten to destroy them.

Beware of Angels is shared with the hope that it will open the eyes of God's commandment-keeping people before it is too late.

Roger Morneau is the author of the Incredible Answers to Prayer series and *A Trip Into the Supernatural*.

US$9.99 / CAN$14.99

ISBN 0-8280-1300-4

REVIEW AND HERALD®
PUBLISHING ASSOCIATION